Endorsements

"**Cultivating Trust** was conceived by love, gestated in experience, and delivered through prayer. On each page, Rebecca pours out her heart through insightful experiences and wisdom, gleaned from her many roles as wife, mother, entrepreneur, teacher, writer, communicator, and, above all, woman of God. She shares transparently from her own struggles, to open truths that will challenge your mindsets. She poses questions to reveal hidden motives while declaring heartfelt prayers that redeem and restore. As I journey with my financial coaching clients, I find myself examining my own spending motives, struggling to release possessive money tendencies, to ultimately find freedom in the knowledge that God owns it all and that I am a privileged manager for a time. **Cultivating Trust** will expose motivations in how you relate to money and contend with mindsets that rob you of abundant life. It is an excellent resource for guiding individual or group money journeys, for counselling couples for marriage, and for financial coaching. This book is a must-read for anyone who seeks financial freedom—you will pleasantly find the true treasure of trusting God in all things."

Natalie Rowe
Human Resources Professional, Financial Coach, and Author

"On the market today, an abundance of books about money exist. Covering subjects such as budgeting, possible financial pitfalls, and money management, few grapple with the heart issues that often underlie our views, beliefs, and habits in terms of how we spend our money and, ultimately, impact our relationship with our Heavenly Father. In her book, **Cultivating Trust**, Rebecca van Noppen deals with those underlying heart issues in a beautiful and relevant way.

Gleaning from the seasons of her life, biblical examples, other authors, musicians, and insights, Rebecca reveals her fears, pain, struggles, joys, and freedoms gained by a willingness to 'go there.' Opening her heart to the tender care of a loving, all-embracing and forgiving Father, He gently guides her and casts light and insight into what to do, pray, or hope for.

Rebecca offers observations, practical applications, and life experiences that cause her relatable words to come alive. Her words are invitational, as Jesus' were, appealing to us to explore and take a deeper dive into one's own heart. The journey leads to examining motivations and long held beliefs, fears, and anxieties that have impacted our intimacy with our Father God and our finances.

Enjoy the journey with Rebecca and experience a heart change!"

Rev. Ray Borg
Ministry & Church Liaison,
Financial Discipleship Canada

"If you want to live a life of 'more than enough,' this practical guide will lead the way.

For many years I have followed the path that Rebecca so clearly lays out in this book. Many of those years, I journeyed this road with her and her husband David; together we helped others do the same. The principles have become a way of life for me and, without question, have given me the courage to step out of the boat and rely on God as never before. Rebecca has captured the fundamental truth that lays the foundation for an abundant life, available to all who follow Jesus."

Lynn Fraser
Co-Founder, More Than Enough Financial Coaching

"If this book has come to your attention, believe that you are called to read it. While this book of devotions is indeed about finances and your perspective on money, it is so much more. It will encourage and help you to cultivate a deeper communication with God, and will bring you face to face with Jesus. As you turn the pages you will journey away from worry and fear towards trust and intimacy with God. You will discover, or rediscover, that God IS our 'more than enough' and, through the provision of Jesus' love, you will find freedom, hope, joy, and so much more. Rebecca van Noppen is a gifted thinker, writer, and teacher. The words come directly from her heart and reflect her personal experience with money, with life, with worry, and with our Lord."

Jennifer Parr
Executive Leadership Coach,
Leadership That Matters

REBECCA van NOPPEN

Cultivating

TRUST

FINDING GOD'S HOPE AND FREEDOM
FOR YOUR FINANCES

YAIRUS PUBLISHING HOUSE
YAIRUS.COM

1   21

FIRST PRINT EDITION
CULTIVATING TRUST
© 2021 REBECCA VAN NOPPEN
ALL RIGHTS RESERVED.

LIBRARY AND ARCHIVES CANADA DATA
ISBN: 978-1-989456-590

Daylon Clark, Executive Publisher
Daylon Clark, Cover Designer
Tim Bloedow, Editor
Miranda Brown, Editor
Zachary van Noppen, Sketch Artist
Andrea Gaw-Prekob, Photographer
IMAGINETHATEXPRESSION.COM

Employ the spiritual talents, special gifts and abilities given by God, to faithfully serve one another, teaching and blessing each other through everything you do for His ultimate Kingdom. Our view on 1 Peter 4:10.

Dedication

All the courageous "soul" farmers and coaching clients: You dig deep to cultivate your financial lives in the Lord. Your commitment and perseverance is inspiring.

Our More Than Enough financial coaches: You give of yourselves tirelessly. Always learning. Always listening. Always asking clarifying questions! Thank you for serving the Lord the way you do!

David: You are the rock God has put in my life to love me for such a time as this. Thank you for everything, always.

My bounty:
Mercedes and Šarūnas, Zachary and Melissa, Hope, Justus, and Serena. You came to your Dad and me in just the right times and seasons. You are gifts and I love you.

"Blessed is the one who trusts in the Lord, whose confidence is in him. They will be like a tree planted by the water that sends out its roots by the stream. It does not fear when heat comes; its leaves are always green. It has no worries in a year of drought and never fails to bear fruit."

JEREMIAH 17:7,8 (NIV)

I saw a tree by the riverside one day as I walked along.
Straight as an arrow and pointing to the sky
growing tall and strong.
"How do you grow so tall and strong?" I said to the riverside tree.
This is the song my tree friend sang to me:

I've got roots growing down to the water,
I've got leaves growing up to the sunshine,
And the fruit that I bear is a sign of the life in me.
I am shade from the hot summer sundown.
I am nest for the birds of the heavens.
I'm becoming what the Lord of trees has meant me to be:

A strong young tree.

FROM "THE TREE SONG" BY KEN MEDEMA

Table of Contents

FOREWARD

CULTIVATING TRUST IN GOD IN THE AREA OF MONEY

As a financial coach for the last 13 years, journeying with hundreds of families including my own, I cannot think of a more relevant topic to contemplate, meditate on, discuss, and digest.

What does the God of the universe say about money, worry, and living life in the 21st century in North America? So much. We can just look to His Word to find over 2,350 verses that pertain to money, financial legacy, and possessions. They are as important for us today as when they were written. *Cultivating Trust* is a relevant reflection of what is found in God's Word. This book is for every Canadian who worries that there will not be enough, whether that is for today, tomorrow, or further into the future. I can think of no better person to be your guide and fellow financial sojourner than Rebecca van Noppen. (Of course, I do have a bit of a bias:-)!)

Rebecca and I have been married for 30 years and have raised five children together. We have lived on no-income, one-income and double-income. We have laughed and cried, worried and persevered, and have walked through each day trusting that our "YES" to the leading of our heavenly Father is all we need for this life—and the one to come.

I am so proud of you, Rebecca. No one knows better than me how much of yourself you have poured into these words. Rebecca does not write as an expert but as one who, as we have lived, prayed, confessed, and changed over time, is able to articulate some of the questions, struggles, and victories that we have experienced.

I want to invite you into this journey. Take time as you read this book. It will churn up the soil of your soul. It has the potential to produce in you a life that is free from worry and stuff, and makes room for heaven to shine through the way you use money. In this world, there is so much need for people to see that **it is possible** to live free from worry and anxiety. The time is now to dig into cultivating trust, allowing the bright light of the Gospel to shine out of your life and light up the world. It is such good news! There is a God who is alive and active in this world to loose the chains of injustice and to untie the chords of debt. He wants to share food, clothes, shelter, and healing with all those He has made. The wonderfully scary part of this is that God uses US to accomplish those things here on earth as they are already established in heaven.

Cultivating Trust will give you an honest, practical, and transparent view of money and how the words of Jesus, the prophets, and the history of the people of God are relevant for today. It is a book where each chapter will deposit seeds that may spring to life immediately or rest dormant for a time and, then, slowly emerge into daily habits and beliefs about money and God that will lead you to partner with God to bring His Kingdom here on earth.

Not only will you hear some of the story of our life, but you will hear words from people who have impacted our life and churned up the soil of our souls, as individuals, as a couple, and as a family. This book reflects some of the fruit that Rebecca is excited to share with you.

I encourage you to take the teaching and the practical exercises and work through them, linger with what provokes you, open your heart and your wallet, and allow the Spirit of God to change your life. This is not a book that you will read once and then put on the shelf. It is a book that you will find yourself referencing over and over again.

Let the journey continue ...

DAVID VAN NOPPEN
CHIEF STEWARDSHIP OFFICER, MORE THAN ENOUGH FINANCIAL

PREFACE
UNLEASHED FOR THE KINGDOM

Unleashed—to be set free from restraints, to release or loose from a restraint or leash.

Unleashed. Set free. Into something more—that no longer binds, pulls down, or hinders.

Into something more—that releases calling, purpose, hope, light, love, and freedom itself.

In 2016, my husband David and I had serious conversations about how to encourage our financial coaching clients at More Than Enough Financial Fitness (MTE), to see that their financial journeys were closely linked to their discipleship journeys with Christ. While the practical one-on-one coaching offered practice, accountability, help, and hope in daily cash flow management, there was a gap. We wanted to tackle the idea that our beliefs and behaviour around money have very little to do with the tool of money itself. It's about the heart and what has our heart's attention. As Jesus once said, we can't serve God and mammon. We will either love the one and hate the other, or be loyal to one and despise the other. We can't serve two masters (see Matthew 6:24).

As we talked, we recognised that there was so much material out there around finances that we questioned whether we really needed to "reinvent the wheel." Couldn't we use a Bible study program that already existed? Did we need to do something more?

The more we talked and prayed, though, the more we felt God wanted to use David and me to express His truths in a way that was unique to the DNA of More Than Enough. We knew we weren't going to say anything new, but we would be obedient, and pray that God would use money issues, financial discussions, and His truth to draw people closer to His heart. We prayed He would use what came to be known as *Unleashed*, to call people back to Himself.

So began a journey of creating 12 workshops that would tackle the heart issues around money. Money stories, purpose, commitment, coveting and contentment, entitlement, stewardship, and generosity are among the topics that small groups engage in on their *Unleashed* journeys.

It was at the end of a three-day brainstorming session for these workshops when David and I watched a Right Now Media video called *Unleashed*.*[1] It was a huge encouragement from the Lord that we were on a good track for creating what He wanted. It was also His reminder to us that this journey of financial discovery in coaching is about freedom. In Galatians, the Lord says that it is for freedom that we are set free so don't get all tangled up again (see Galatians 5:1). The word unleashed and the Right Now Media video, *Unleashed*, beautifully encapsulate that verse; and so the workshops were named. Since 2017, we have run *Unleashed* small groups both in person and online.

Unleashed from Worry into Cultivated Trust

This book that you hold has been birthed out of *Unleashed*. It also comes at a time when worry, anxiety, and fear have been heightened by sickness, death, job loss, and growing national debt in the face of Covid-19.

People are afraid and are worried about tomorrow. The days are uncertain, but, truly, they are no less troublesome than they were 2,000 years ago when Rome dominated much of the known world. It is my hope that you will find practical help from the words of Jesus Christ, as well as His comfort, as you hear Him speak His truth: "Do not worry about tomorrow, about what you will eat or drink. Our Heavenly Father knows what you need even before you ask. Do you not know that you are more valuable than the birds of the sky or the flowers of the field?" (see Matthew 6). The times may change, but His words and His truth don't.

*To watch the *Unleashed* video that inspired the naming of the workshops, refer to the link below. The words from the video are also written below.

UNLEASHED RIGHT NOW MEDIA VIDEO
https://www.youtube.com/watch?v=6YnG3jFkJwU&t=2s

The sun rose and work began. Word of a better day spread throughout the people. A day free from bondage. This hope carried them through their labour. They knew their God was faithful. That he had a plan. One to set them free to a land promised by God—to His people, for His people. A plan of redemption. But they lost focus—turned away from the God who is faithful. Worshiped false idols. Turned back to the very culture God was rescuing them from. Turned back to their past—to bondage.

So they wandered and wandered. They began to grumble and curse the God who rescued them. They would never set foot in the land they were promised. They would never be Unleashed. But God's plan perseveres despite the disobedience of His people. He waited for a new generation to rise up from the dust, one that would step out from their wandering and into the purpose for which God was calling them. To be a nation set apart that would bring glory to Him.

He continues to call those courageous followers out of the desert, away from our wanderings to be God's representatives here on earth: to be released from the bondage of our past, from being brainwashed by culture. Unleashed with the backbone to lead the church. Unleashed with the boldness to serve the world. Unleashed for the Gospel. He calls His people to be Unleashed.

Introduction

"Can any one of you by worrying add a single hour to your life?"

MATTHEW 6:27 (NIV)

"Blessed is the one who trusts in the Lord, whose confidence is in him. They will be like a tree planted by the water that sends out its roots by the stream. It does not fear when heat comes; its leaves are always green. It has no worries in a year of drought and never fails to bear fruit."

JEREMIAH 17:7,8 (NIV)

We are in the midst of a global pandemic. Actually, the anniversary of our first shut down is only a few weeks away as I write this. It has been a long year, but the days have seemed short. We live in a beautiful Canadian space and our children have been with us. Our daily work at MTE has been full and meaningful, although challenging. I have been homeschooling our youngest, ten-year-old Serena, managing our *Let's Talk Money with Dave and Reb* podcast, and administering our coaching program at MTE. So much good has come out of this time, but I am continually aware of the individual and community levels of worry, anxiety, and fear so many of us are experiencing.

People have health concerns, but they also have financial concerns. As we try to manage the spread of Covid-19, people are losing their jobs, businesses are closing, and individual, family, and national debt levels are increasing. Some have been able to save more money as they work from home but, overall, financial worries are prevalent.

As I write about Jesus' teaching in Matthew 6, I am aware of our MTE vision statement—Hope for Today, Freedom for Tomorrow. This is what we do. We do our best to encourage people practically and spiritually to walk in hope and freedom, both in their finances and in their overall Christian lives. David, our MTE head financial coach, says debt isn't a sin but it is a burden and a weight. Financial coaching is the practical way in which we try to bring people hope that financial freedom is possible. The times may change, but Jesus and His words don't change. He is the hope in our worry, and the freedom from it. He tells us continually to trust Him for He is good and loving and kind.

At MTE, and through our *Unleashed* coaching program, our team will tell you that we don't have money, worry, and trust all figured out. In fact, this weekend I am admonished again to keep focused on Jesus Christ alone in the midst of pandemic numbers and hard stories that our friends are walking through. However, I am here. I am writing these words to you as a companion, a guide, and a friend, leading you to the greatest hope and friend and companion you can find—Jesus.

Please note—and this is my confession—I still worry. I still get anxious. But I am quicker to come to Him than I used to come. I find I worry less as I process the emotions of worry and fear with my family and friends. I worry less as I consciously choose every day to spend time with God. I worry less as I choose to trust. I keep learning just like you do, and I am learning to take the words of Matthew 6 more and more seriously.

Come what may, God the Father, Jesus His Son, and our guide Holy Spirit is trustworthy; more trustworthy than the worry that cannot add a cubit to my lifespan. I pray that you and I will be freed daily from the worry that strips us of life, love, and joy, especially as we remember the words of Christ—worry doesn't add anything to our lives.

THE IRONY

The irony for me in writing this during the global pandemic, is that when I am tired and spent after days of working hard, navigating our life, and having a writing deadline, I find myself increasingly susceptible to worry. As my family knows, it is during these moments I try to gain more and more control of the circumstances, demanding more of myself and them. It never looks pretty. This morning, David graciously reminded me that in these moments, I need to remember my default wiring to try and control outcomes. He reminded me that God will help me with the words I write, with the MTE work I do, and with loving those around me. I know in my head that I cannot control outcomes. I don't run the universe, but somehow in my default position, it always makes me feel better to have order in some areas of my life, especially when there are life stories and events I cannot change. Sometimes the anxiety, fear, and fatigue that drive me to create that order damage relationships, so I continue to learn. David and I, and our kids, keep talking about my responses and reactions, and theirs too. I am thankful for a family who is in this with me.

I don't know what it looks like in your world when worry and anxiety, particularly over finances, come knocking on your door. Perhaps during our journey together through these pages, you will start to see those places more clearly. It is my hope that you invite God into all of those spaces—the ugly and the controlling, the beautiful and the trusting. He is always with you. Your invitation to Him is simply a reminder that He is near, closer than you realize. As writer and theologian Henri Nouwen writes in his book *Home Tonight,* our Heavenly Father isn't just waiting for our return from the worries, fears, and prodigal living that assail us. He is with us as we leave and turn away into our worries and fears. "I believe the Giver of Life loves each of us as a daughter or a son who is leaving and returning constantly. The more we become sensitive to our own journey the more we realize that we are leaving and coming back every day, every hour."[1] God, our Father, isn't only with us when we are returning from our troubles, but He is with us as we head into them.

HOW TO USE THIS BOOK—A BOOK OF MUTUAL INVITATION
In the pages that follow, it is my hope that you hear your Creator calling to you by name. It is my hope that you hear the invitation of Jesus, calling you to come to Him and lay your worries down, to learn of Him, and to trust Him more deeply. It is also my hope that you do some inviting yourself. Invite God into those places where you are worried and afraid. Invite Him to be your provision even when you don't

understand why your journey feels as hard as it does. As you journey together, you will find opportunities to respond to His invitation and discover how He is responding to you.

You can read through the chapters in "one fell swoop."* Or you can work at them slowly, applying the Cultivating Communion sections for deeper understanding and application. In some of the chapters, I have also included examples of how you can respond to God. It is my hope that as you read these pages, you will find practical tips and tools, as well as heart lessons in your journey with God. I earnestly believe that if our journeys with God and money were only about the money, and getting more education, we wouldn't have the personal and national debt loads we are seeing around the world. We also would know how to talk about money without fighting with our spouse, and we would be open-handed in generosity. There are so many resources, books, podcasts, and teaching webinars out there that we don't have any excuses for not knowing enough. It's all there for us to find and learn. From what David and I have seen in the Canadian community we serve, this is not about more education. We need heart transformation and fresh, counter-cultural, solid biblical money management habits when it comes to taking care of our finances. This is why we believe so strongly in the financial coaching process, and why we believe that community is key to keeping us accountable and heading in the right direction.

In terms of using this book, you may find it helpful to read through it first, and then go back and start working through the Cultivating Communion sections. You may want to work through it as an individual, but also meet weekly with a small group to talk about what you have learned. In other words, use this in the way that best suits your learning style, your needs, and the season you are in. You may find you can only work through one chapter a week and that works too. There is no right or wrong way to walk this journey. It is your journey. So listen to God's Spirit direct you through it.

A NOTE ABOUT WORSHIP AND PRAISE MUSIC

I am not sure how it happened, but a few of the Cultivating Communion sections involve listening to worship and praise music. This has actually taken me a bit by surprise! I love music and, back in the day, I led worship teams in our Christian community. I grew up singing in choirs and competing in music festivals. I guess it shouldn't surprise me that music has come to play a part in the writing of this book, and in the practical applications of some of the truths laid out here. I hope you take the time to listen and be still, just as I did as I wrote.

*This means to do something all at once, or very suddenly, and comes from one of Shakespeare's writings in 1605: *Macbeth* (Act 4, Scene 3). For more information you can visit https://www.dailywritingtips.com/one-fell-swoop/.

Prayers for the Journey

"Fear not, for I am with you; be not dismayed for I am your God.
I will strengthen you,
Yes, I will help you,
I will uphold you with my righteous right hand."

ISAIAH **41:10 (NKJV)**

Dearest Father, Blessed Son, Vibrant Spirit,

We come to You at the beginning of this journey, seeking Your wisdom, acknowledging as we do so that You are our Wisdom, our Hope, and our Trust.

Thank You for Your promises that strengthen us, Your presence that helps us, and Your power and love that uphold us. We come into Your Presence now with thankful hearts, seeking Your face, Your wisdom, and knowing the goodness and the depth of love You have for us. Thank You for the riches we have through Christ Jesus our Lord that enable us to call You Abba, Saviour, Lord, and Friend.

By Your Word we are held together. From You there is nothing hidden. We come, inviting You into the story of our lives, knowing that You are ever present with us. Thank You that You never leave us or forsake us. Thank You that You are with us in our leaving and in our returning. You are our ever present help in times of trouble, an eternal guiding force of love and hope in the midst of the ebb and flow of our lives.

We need You. We are desperate for You. We ask, as we begin our journey into deeper trust with You, that You meet us and do the unseen work of transformation we cannot do for ourselves. As we come to learn to rest in Your trusting presence, abiding in Your truth, Your ways, and in Your love, we will wait on You for Your timing; Your completion of what our hearts need most.

As we cultivate the soil of our hearts to receive the seed of Your transforming words, grant us Your joy that renews us, Your hope that propels us, and Your love that secures us. We receive Your grace and peace, through Jesus Christ, our Lord. Amen.

"Against the Love of Money," a prayer from the *Common Prayer Pocket Edition*[1]

Once again, Lord Jesus Christ, I face the power of avarice.

Against the torrent of oblivion, I plead the blood of Jesus.

When I worry about survival and grasp for false security, remind me of the boy who shared his meal so you could feed the multitudes.

When I am tempted to store up treasure in savings accounts, help me to make eternal investments in your kingdom and trust your economy of love.

When I wonder who will care for me when I am old, give me elders to love and young friends to mentor in your way of abundant life.

Deliver me from avarice, that I might know the love that casts out fear and receive the gift of your provision through another's hand.

Lord Jesus Christ, Son of God, have mercy on me, a sinner.

Cultivating Trust

"We will never truly trust God with our lives if we can't trust Him with our finances. In some sense, the last thing to be saved is our wallets—and until that happens we have never fully surrendered."

DAVE FROESE, TENDER FRUIT GROWER,
NIAGARA-ON-THE-LAKE, ONTARIO

"Be patient, then, brothers and sisters, until the Lord's coming. See how the farmer waits for the land to yield its valuable crop, patiently waiting for the autumn and spring rains. You too, be patient and stand firm, because the Lord's coming is near."

JAMES 5:7-8 (NIV)

Cultivating Trust—Finding God's Hope and Freedom for Your Finances. What does this term "cultivating" have to do with trusting God? And what does cultivating trust have to do with our finances?

Cultivation has a broad scope of meaning that encompasses agricultural work, education, growth, and relational development. Cultivation involves preparing and working land in order to raise crops. It involves tilling the soil and improves the growth of a plant or crop. A person cultivates through education and training, and thereby promotes the growth or development of goals, tasks, or pursuits in everyday life. Cultivation can also mean fostering or devoting oneself to something, as well as seeking and developing friendship.

When it comes to cultivating trust with God in our finances, all of these definitions apply. We are preparing and working the soil of our hearts by spending time with Him to grow the seeds of trust and faithfulness He has planted. We pay attention to these seeds and soil so it doesn't get overrun with weeds, and we also devote ourselves to

God in order to cultivate and foster deep friendship with Him. This involves all the aspects of cultivation as we learn, grow, and develop relationship.

From an agricultural perspective, this word "cultivating" is rich in meaning as we apply it to trusting God in our financial lives. Farming is not for cowards, and neither is developing trust in God. Both demand our dependence and reliance on what is outside of ourselves to control. While a farmer works hard to prepare the fields through planning, cultivating, and planting, they also depend on weather patterns, rainfall, sunshine, and the quality of the seeds to bring every meal to our table. In the same way, as hard as we work at providing for ourselves through planning, determination, and good money management, we are also dependent on God in the challenges, adversities, and troubles that are a part of life.

> "FARMING IS NOT FOR COWARDS, AND NEITHER IS DEVELOPING TRUST IN GOD. BOTH DEMAND OUR DEPENDENCE AND RELIANCE ON WHAT IS OUTSIDE OF OURSELVES TO CONTROL."

My brother Dave Froese, who is 19 years my senior, has been cultivating farmland for over 55 years. He could have long since been retired, but he loves his calling and vocation so much I don't think he will ever stop. He has lived through the ups and downs of farming life, including hail storms, early frosts, drought, excessive rain, and two devastating barn fires in 1991 and 1997. With his hand firmly in the hand of God, Dave has persevered, refusing to give up, and has simply—or not so simply—trusted. His love for farming, and for God, has carried him through these rough patches. I know that as much as my brother loves farming, he loves Jesus more, and it is within these two loves that he finds the joy and challenge to keep cultivating what God has given him. On the land, he sees cultivation as a means of getting rid of weeds, softening the soil for plants to take root, thus invigorating growth. He says cultivating the ground helps it work like a sponge, retaining moisture when it rains.

To my brother, cultivating the ground is just like cultivating the soil of our hearts. "Some of us have really hard ground where God is trying to plant, and we need some work," he says. "Cultivating our relationship with God is like cultivating a relationship with anyone. We need to spend time with Him, trust and believe Him, and receive the truth He speaks to us."

In this process of trusting God with our finances, Dave believes that Christ-followers need to understand that God is the owner of everything and He has promises that He always keeps. "That is like ground zero and we need to get our heads around that first. We also need to believe the promises of God in His Word, or otherwise nothing convinces us to release our finances to God."

Cultivating trust with God in finance doesn't happen on its own. It takes intentionality, time, relationship, knowledge of the truth, and hard work. Just as a farmer ploughs a field, so we walk with God as He turns up the soil of our hearts. He shows us the areas that need cultivating, where the weeds are, and how to carefully watch over the needs of our hearts with grace and compassion.

Our friends Tony and Shelley Spruit started *Against The Grain Farms* just up the road from where we live. Born into a generational farm family, Shelley grew up doing chores and milking cows, and her teenage summers were spent working on farms. She has now worked farmland with Tony for 34 years. On occasion, I walk with her through her grain fields. I listen to her words and her heart, and am left astounded at the passion she has for the land, the grain, and the Lord she loves. Imagine yourself walking with her on a warm and windy day, and listen as she speaks about cultivating trust:

Cultivation is unique for different crops, soil types, and seasons. I thought "wow, that is exactly how God sees each of us". In His hands, some of us have areas of clay, or sandy loam, and then there are other areas in our life that are just pure cement! We, as follow-ers of Christ, also cultivate our relationship with God differently depending on our season of life and what specifically we are trying to grow. Right now, I am so struck by the absolute beauty of the Estonia rye in our field. It is well over seven feet tall, planted on a rocky ridge, with no fertilizers and a serious shortage of rain. To me, this is a mature Christian who has dug his roots into the soils of life, and, no matter what the storms of life are, they stand firm, resilient, and beautiful.

There is also a way of farming today that diverges from the old theory of working the soil before planting. Shelley compares this "no-till" agriculture to waiting before the Lord. For Shelley, this too is another way of cultivating trust:

> More and more, we are realizing that with regenerative agriculture it is best not to work the soil as it causes too much water loss, nutrient loss, and the breakdown of the microbial activity that is going on underground. Cultivating our relationship with God often means learning to be a Mary instead of a Martha; more is not always better. Waiting, listening, and praying are like the realization that "no-till", with little disturbance of the soil, is better than big heavy equipment constantly turning over the soil. I try to look at nature as a means of learning how to cultivate trust in God. It is, after all, God's visual word to us. As the saying goes, "Have patience! In time, even grass becomes milk." We plant a seed, we cultivate and keep the weeds out, but then we wait in trust that the rains and the sun will come. Likewise with God, I am learning the importance of letting the seasons mature the seeds of life.

Cultivating Trust—Finding God's Hope and Freedom for Your Finances. This will take commitment, intention, and waiting. Sometimes it will mean turning up the soil of our hearts to expose our limited beliefs about God and ourselves. Sometimes it will mean churning, planting, and then waiting for the fruit to mature, as we grow in understanding of His provision, promises, and care for us. Sometimes, this trust will involve simply walking the land of our hearts and talking to the Lord about what He is planting there—without the churning and pulling—so that we grow in greater understanding of the One who loves us and gave Himself for us.

We are always cultivating trust. If it is not in the Lord, then it is in our own abilities to work and manage money. If it is not in the Lord, then it may be in our bank accounts, our access to credit, or in a family member's ability to bail us out. I am sure there are other places we put our trust when it comes to money, and I have been discovering them in my own heart over these years. This is why I have written this book. I want to put my trust in my Creator God.

Every.
Single.
Day.

I want that for you too. Scripture says in Psalm 20:7, "Some trust in chariots and some in horses, but we trust in the name of the Lord our God" (NIV). Let's learn how to do that, together.

With God

"You will love me if you do what I say."
Jesus

I am gripped by this statement today.

If I love Him, I will do what He says. As a Christian, I have heard that all of my life. For many years those words strangled my relationship with Him because I felt His love was conditional on my obedience. It felt like He just wanted me to fulfill all the "dos and don'ts" of Christian life: "Do what I say and I will love you."

It took me many years to undo that thinking, and I am not sure I completely grasp it yet. I know I can't attain holiness on my own, but some days I still grapple with the truth that God loves me unconditionally no matter what I've done. His acceptance of me and His love are not based on my ability to fulfill the law, and that is still astounding to me.

I remember when my kids were younger and we were homeschooling, I had a sign in the schoolroom that said, "Huff Less, Do More." This came out of complaints I kept hearing about school work. The complaining slowed the process of learning and drove me a bit crazy. Eventually, I changed my philosophy and the words of that school room sign. I realized I was creating "doers" and "worker bees" because I was so focused on obedience and getting the work done. I am so glad something within me shifted. The sign changed and instead of *doing* more, I encouraged more love—love of each other; love of learning. As they loved and learned, I was hoping the desire to complete the work would grow. "Huff Less, Love and Obey More" became the sign. We laugh at those signs today, but they are words that continue to ring in my head!

This brings me back to a question I keep asking myself about why people—why Christ-followers—have such a hard time staying out of debt and living a life free from worldly attachments, when we KNOW that Jesus has shown us a different way to live. He taught and modelled His life after a heart of love and obedience to His Father. Do I—do we—truly love Him? Jesus wants our hearts. Unattached. He clearly tells us we cannot serve God while serving money, possessions, and the ways of mammon. So why do I serve money and stuff, and the things the world loves, when Jesus clearly warns me about that? His warning is explicit: If I hate the one, I will love the other. If I am devoted to one, I will despise the other (see Matthew 6:24-25).

I think there are many reasons why we serve money and stuff rather than God, and all of them have to do with our heart's motivations and what we truly want and love. Every person has their own story, and their own reasons. This is not new revelation and may be stating the obvious. As Paul says in Romans 7, I keep doing the things I don't want to do, knowing full well they are not good for me. Yet, I keep doing them anyway. Paul is verbalizing a frustration that we can all identify with. Saying, teaching, and writing the words are a lot easier than *living out* Christ's calling to love God first and serve Him only. There are so many enticements in our world calling us to a different, wider path. But you know what? I keep hearing Him calling me to return to His grace, His love, and His acceptance, even when I fall short of the mark. He welcomes me again and again as I struggle through the temptations and the mechanical obedience. He keeps calling me back to Himself and I keep returning, sometimes battered and bruised, sometimes rejoicing. I return especially in those times when my heart is overwhelmed by all the "doing." I come and I fall at His feet because I know that I cannot keep up with the doings of His Word and His commands without loving Him most. So I come to His feet. I crumple in a heap. I hear Him speak. I feel Him reach out to me with His nail pierced hands and say, "Stand up. Go on. Love like I love. You are not alone. I know you serve yourself sometimes, but keep turning back. Keep turning back to Me and I will fill you with what you need. Remember who I am. Remember who you are. Walk with Me, and practice one thing every day that will keep you focused and set on Me."

If I haven't realized it yet, this is an invitation into communion with Him. He is inviting me again and again to commune with Him in the doing and the being, in the working and the waiting. Author, pastor, and speaker Skye Jethani from *The Holy Post* podcast says it is more than just focusing on the *being* of discipleship or the *doing* of discipleship. It is expanding our understanding of the Mary and Martha story. In one of *The Holy Post* podcasts, he says that whether we are in quiet moments with God in prayer and stillness or in moments of active obedience, we are to do them rooted in God's presence. "I don't like the dichotomy of 'be' versus 'do'...Rather than 'be' versus 'do,' we should talk about 'be with' or 'do with.'"[1] He encourages disciples to *be with God*, **and** *do with God,* and this brings us back to the beginning.

"If you love me you will do what I say."

Today, it might be cooking for my neighbour. Tomorrow, it may mean keeping my credit card at home. The next day, it may be making more space in my day to discover Jesus in His Word. The day after that, it may be sharing my worries about money with a trusted friend. This is being and doing with God—in communion, in His presence. It is loving every day, together with Him.

So what do these thoughts have to do with freedom from worry and seeking His Kingdom? Discipleship and communion exist within the surrendered journey of trusting God. It is where we discover more of God, more of His heart, and more of what matters to Him. The fruit of this communion will be a deeper trust with God in our finances.

MEDITATE: DEUTERONOMY 6:1-9, JEREMIAH 2:11-13

CULTIVATING COMMUNION

Our *being* and our *doing* flows out of our communion with God. Our life flows from Him as our Source. A group of pastoral students were asked once if they spent much of their time reading the Gospels to learn more about Christ, to draw closer to Him. Perhaps it wouldn't surprise you that in that educational setting, many students were reading the Gospels simply as course material. The question then turns to you and me: how are we reading the Gospels? A life of communion with God is going to bear all kinds of fruit, in your life and mine. As we dig into cultivating trust with God in finance, it is my prayer that fruit will grow in you and that you will desire to know Christ more and more.

True discipleship and communion does involve obedience. Do you find obeying God in your finances a challenge? Think about a time when you obeyed God in your finances. This could be obedience in giving, saving first before you bought, paying a bill, or asking for help. On the other hand, can you think of a time when you struggled to obey, or didn't obey? What happened and how did you feel? Reflect and consider how both of those situations have affected your relationship with God. Are you closer now because of them? Have you learned to trust Him more with your money? Or do you keep your money a "hidden" topic when it comes to God and prayer? Take some time now to talk with Him about where these stories of worry and trust have brought you, and where you would like these stories to take you in the future; a place where you are unleashed into deeper trust.

God is My Jehovah Jireh

The theme of God being my Provider is one that has run consistently throughout my life. I have so many stories to tell in this regard, that a book would never hold them all. However, I will highlight a few here.

One story that significantly stands out is the whirlwind year I dated Ray. We began to date on November 14th, 1987, became engaged in early January of 1988, married five months later on June 18th, and by August were unexpectedly pregnant. Ray and I were in shock. Ray had recently graduated with a Master's Degree in Social Work and still carried a significant level of debt. I had always felt that I needed to be home with my babies if I ever became a mom. We looked at each other and decided to pare down our lifestyle to live on Ray's salary alone. We felt like we literally "lived on pennies" but, praise God, by the time our precious and beloved daughter arrived in April of 1989, we had paid off $25,000 of school debt and were debt free! We felt like it was a miracle and praised God for His help.

Another significant story is when Ray sensed his time at the Children's Aid Society (CAS) had come to an end. His final year at CAS was one of high stress and responsibility, overseeing a budget of 30 million dollars. His hair had turned grey that year, and we knew it was time for a new season. After discussing many options, with no decision and no plan, to the great worry of many family and friends who loved us, Ray's time at CAS ended on May 31st, 2008. Three days later, to the utter amazement and joy of everyone, especially Ray and me, he received a call from a friend who owned a company and knew our story. She offered Ray a job as a Human Resources Consultant. How we all rejoiced and praised God over His incredible provision! Ray worked with this company for the next six years.

An old classic song, "Jehovah Jireh, My Provider," rings in my spirit even as I am writing these words. The words in Genesis 22:14, "the Lord will provide," are a promise that I have seen God fulfill in my life in a myriad of ways. To Him be the glory forever and ever!

ARLENE BORG
OTTAWA, ONTARIO, 2021

An Invitation

"Taste and See that the Lord is good,
Blessed is the one who takes refuge in Him."

PSALM 34:8 (NIV)

"Ho! Everyone who thirsts,
Come to the waters;
And you who have no money,
Come, buy and eat.
Yes, come, buy wine and milk
Without money and without price.

"Why do you spend money for what is not bread,
And your wages for what does not satisfy?
Listen carefully to Me, and eat what is good,
And let your soul delight itself in abundance.

"Incline your ear, and come to Me.
Hear, and your soul shall live;
And I will make an everlasting covenant with you—
The sure mercies of David."

ISAIAH 55:1-3 (NKJV)

While writing about trusting God and releasing worry, I realize the best advice about worry comes from Jesus in the book of Matthew. What can I say that hasn't first been said by Him? If you go to Matthew 6 and read verses 19 to 34, you will find God's invitation to trust and love Him. It's the invitation I hear echoing from the prophet Isaiah hundreds of years before. Isaiah 55 challenges us to listen carefully to the Source of Life, and eat what is good. He invites us to come, eat, and listen, whether or not we have lots of money. Having money is not a prerequisite for coming to Him or eating at His table. Neither is it a prerequisite for living an abundant life.

So let's take His advice. Let's come to His table and eat what is good. Let's set aside the distractions, the needs, the wants, and the worries. Let's chew on Matthew 6 and Isaiah 55 together. Chew His words, mull them over, and then take another bite. In the days ahead, we will continue our reflections on this passage, but for now, just take in His Words.

Matthew 6:19-34 (NIV)

Do not store up for yourselves treasures on earth, where moths and vermin destroy, and where thieves break in and steal. But store up for yourselves treasures in heaven, where moths and vermin do not destroy, and where thieves do not break in and steal. For where your treasure is, there your heart will be also.

The eye is the lamp of the body. If your eyes are healthy, your whole body will be full of light. But if your eyes are unhealthy, your whole body will be full of darkness. If then the light within you is darkness, how great is that darkness!

No one can serve two masters. Either you will hate the one and love the other, or you will be devoted to the one and despise the other. You cannot serve both God and money.

> HAVING MONEY IS NOT A PREREQUISITE FOR COMING TO HIM OR EATING AT HIS TABLE. NEITHER IS IT A PREREQUISITE FOR LIVING AN ABUNDANT LIFE.

Therefore I tell you, do not worry about your life, what you will eat or drink; or about your body, what you will wear. Is not life more than food, and the body more than clothes? Look at the birds of the air; they do not sow or reap or store away in barns, and yet your heavenly Father feeds them. Are you not much more valuable than they? Can any one of you by worrying add a single hour to your life?

And why do you worry about clothes? See how the flowers of the field grow. They do not labor or spin. Yet I tell you that not even Solomon in all his splendor was dressed like one of these. If that is how God clothes the grass of the field, which is here today and tomorrow is thrown into the fire, will he not much more clothe you—you of little faith? So do not worry, saying, "What shall we eat?" or "What shall we drink?" or "What shall we wear?" For the pagans run after all these things, and your heavenly Father knows that you need them. But seek first his kingdom and his righteousness, and all these things will be given to you as well. Therefore do not worry about tomorrow, for tomorrow will worry about itself. Each day has enough trouble of its own.

MEDITATE: MATTHEW 6:19-34, ISAIAH 55:1-3

CULTIVATING COMMUNION

Take some time to read these passages. You can change it up by listening to each passage through an online app. Perhaps listen to it three different times from three different versions of the Bible to get a clearer understanding. Ponder what jumps out at you. Is there a word, phrase, or verse that speaks to you in this moment?

- Write it down.
- Ask the question of God and yourself why that word is so important.
- Write down any thoughts that come to you.
- Pray and thank God for what He is showing you.
- Ask God how to apply that word to your life today.

For example:

1. **What word or phrase jumps out to me?** Listen carefully to Me and eat what is good from Isaiah 55.
2. **Why is this important for me, Lord?** I have been listening to lots of other voices from social media, family, and friends and haven't spent much time with God lately. I haven't been reading His written Word either.

3. **How do I apply this to my life?** I am going to set my alarm for half an hour earlier than normal tomorrow so I can get up and take some time to pray and be with God in His Word.

What is Worry?

"The Lord is my Shepherd, I lack nothing."
PSALM 23:1 (NIV)

We talk a lot about worry, anxiety, mental health, panic attacks, and stress in our Canadian culture today. Depression, discouragement, despair, and feelings of hopelessness can follow these experiences of worry and anxiety. I am not an expert on worry—other than that I have spent lots of time doing it—so I cannot speak to its many facets and complications. What I can speak to is my own journey with worry and anxiety, and how God has drawn me away from fears and deeper into trust and dependence on Him, especially in my finances.

So if we are going to talk about trust, worry, and finances—what is worry? Worry is the state of anxiety over actual, potential, or perceived problems. If you are living and breathing on planet earth, you have likely felt worried, anxious, or fearful over any number of situations in your life.

Do we need to go far to understand what worry or anxiety look like? We just need to see what is happening in our own bodies when we are under stress. Sometimes we have a fight-or-flight stress response which releases adrenaline into our system. An increased pulse or breathing rate results. In my own body, anxiety feels like pressure on my chest or an inability to think clearly.

When David and I were leaving the family automotive business in 2007, a familiar feeling would sometimes creep into me, or I guess it would creep out of me. My heart sometimes raced and pressure on my chest threatened my thinking. This happened as I considered relationships we were leaving behind, misunderstandings we were experiencing, and the prospects of an unknown and uncertain financial future without a job or income. David and I had each other, and we had the Lord directing us, but it did not erase the feelings of panic that would come. Sometimes, when the thoughts and anxieties about our situation were too much, my heart would race, and I would either want to work harder to try and "fix" the challenges that came along, or I would want to crawl into bed and stay there.

"Therefore I say to you, do not worry about your life," Jesus said (Matthew 6:25, NKJV).

Even as I write these words, read them, and eat this truth of Christ, I am arrested by His words again. *Don't worry.* He once spoke those words in real time to flesh and blood disciples. Today, those words continue to speak into my present story, my messy and sometimes chaotic life, and my own heart and mind. Don't worry.

In Greek, one of the words for worry—"merimnao"—means to be anxious, or to be troubled with cares.[1] This is the word found in Matthew 6, where Jesus teaches us to trust in God's love instead of worrying about our life, provision, and, most specifically, what we will eat and drink.

> WHEN WE FEEL WORRY OR PANIC, WE CAN USE THEM AS RED FLAGS OR SIGNS TO SHOW US THAT SOMETHING IS AMISS. WE CAN USE THESE MOMENTS TO DRAW US TOWARDS GOD, WHERE WE CRY OUT FOR HELP. THIS IS WHAT WORRY CAN TEACH US: IT CAN TEACH US TO TURN TO GOD.

The worry about money comes for many reasons as unique as each human being, but it often comes down to thinking we don't, or won't, have enough. Our worry is often focused on what is to come tomorrow. There is no shame in feeling worried. What Jesus is most concerned about is what we are doing with these responses and emotions. It is one of many reasons why Jesus came to set us free. He wants to show us the way to trusting God. Jesus continually encourages us to NOT be afraid, to NOT worry about tomorrow, and to NOT worry about what we will wear, eat, or drink. It is the way of discipleship to draw closer to the heart of God in the midst of the worries and fears that overwhelm us. When we feel worry or panic, we can use them as red flags or signs to show us that something is amiss. We can use these moments to draw us towards God, where we cry out for help. This is what worry can teach us: it can teach us to turn to God.

MEDITATE: PSALM 23

CULTIVATING COMMUNION
We will chew and digest the words of Jesus found in Matthew 6 in the days ahead, and as we walk from worry and fear to trust and intimacy with God, we want to remember that He is our Good Shepherd.

What do you want from your journey ahead as you learn to cultivate trust and let go of financial worry. Write down or tell God what you are hoping for. Is it transformation? Is it practical help to pay down debt? Is it clearer communication with your spouse around the topic of money? Is it learning who you are, and who God is, so you can learn to trust Him more? Thank Him for the journey you are on, and tell Him your desires.

Now consider that the Lord is Your Shepherd. What does Psalm 23:1-3 mean to you?

The Lord is my shepherd; I shall not want.
He makes me to lie down in green pastures;
He leads me beside the still waters.

He restores my soul;
He leads me in the paths of righteousness
For His name's sake (NKJV).

What truth(s) can you remind yourself of when you start to worry about your finances? Write it (them) down, and give a prayer of thanks for this provision of truth.

What Are You Worried About?

"Don't worry. Which of you by worrying can add even an inch to your life? So, why are you worrying? Consider the lilies. Look at the birds. Look at the grass, you of little faith. Consider. Look. Watch. Don't worry."

JESUS, PARAPHRASED FROM MATTHEW 6:30-32

So. What are you worried about?

After 12 years as a financial coach, my husband David says that a lot of the stress and worry he sees in people comes from the "extras" we want, not necessarily the "needs" that Jesus is talking about in Matthew 6. The difference, he says, arises between "perceived" needs and "actual" needs. Maybe it's not the gas we need to fill the car, but the $1,000 phone we want, or think we need, that is causing us stress. That being said, worrying about what we eat, what we drink, or what we wear, is also an issue. If it wasn't, Jesus would never have said anything about it.

"Therefore I say to you, do not worry about your life, what you will eat or what you will drink; nor about your body, what you will put on. Is not life more than food and the body more than clothing?" (Matthew 6:25, NKJV.)

At the base level of life, we need food, water, clothing, shelter, and loving relationships. In 1943, American psychologist Abraham Harold Maslow depicted these needs in a triangular scale.[1] The bottom tier represents physiological needs, then climbing upward, the tiers include safety needs, belonging needs like intimate relationships, esteem needs like accomplishment, and self-fulfillment needs like creativity. The triangle came to be known as Maslow's Hierarchy of Needs.[2]

We all experience needs, of course. Some of Maslow's are ones we fulfill without experiencing worry. Others, however, cause us great stress.

Take my parents for instance. When Jacob and Tina Froese started their life together, they would not necessarily have thought a lot about their dreams because they were busy on the bottom rung of Maslow's triangle, taking care of food, water, shelter, and clothing. They were farmers and, consequently, provided their seven children with lots of food, the secure shelter of the farm house, and the land they cultivated. In terms of this triangle, they started at the bottom, but they began moving towards self-fulfillment as the years progressed. My father came to a place where he could both farm and fulfill a dream of entering political life. He eventually became Lord Mayor of Niagara-on-the-Lake and hosted Queen Elizabeth II in 1973. He then turned to federal politics, becoming a Member of Parliament in 1979. Growing up he had heard the words that he would *"never amount to much,"* but, in the end, he accomplished his purpose in a way that an uneducated man might not dream of today. I tell you this story because their lives were not without worry. In fact, my Dad suffered the pain of incredible migraines because of the stress and worry some of these "needs" brought into his life. The years running a construction business before turning to farming didn't help either. It took many years for my Dad to release financial anxieties and life-stressors to God, but He did, and his story is what encourages me to keep going on the hard days.

My mom and dad are both now with Jesus. When I am struggling to trust God with my financial story, I remember their stories, and I realize how fast 90 years goes by. When David left the family business, and we weren't earning much income, my mom said these words to me and they have never left me: "When you are 80-years-old, you are not going to look back on your life and remember all those grocery trips where you didn't have enough money to buy what you wanted. You just won't be thinking that way. So don't worry so much. You have what you need. God will always take care of you."

So sometimes, when I sense that my worries are taking me down that unprofitable path of thought, I picture myself as an 80-year-old woman reflecting on my life and I remember my mother's words. I imagine myself thinking about my life, and I am not thinking about groceries!

MEDITATE: MATTHEW 6:30-32

CULTIVATING COMMUNION
What about you? What will you remember when you are 80? Having my mother's perspective can help each of us not get overwhelmed by what faces us today.

So, what is troubling you? Jesus reminds us and reinforces again and again in Matthew 6 that we are not to worry. Why? Because our Heavenly Father loves us and cares for us more than He does for the birds of the air. He knows that we need food, water, and clothing. We can trust Him to take care of us.

What are some of the needs in your life? Draw a line down the middle of a journal page. On one side write "perceived needs" and on the other write "actual needs." Start making a list. Maybe you can even do this with a friend or family member. This is a great way to raise awareness about what you need, what you want, and what is causing the worry. Of these "needs" what, if any, are the ones you spend time worrying about? Circle those in red. For instance, food is a need we all have, and buying groceries can cause us anxiety when we see prices rising when our income is not. After you circle those areas that cause you worry, bring them to God in prayer and ask Him to show you how to trust Him.

At More Than Enough we like to encourage people to **FACE** their finances. This is an acronym for **F**inancial **A**wareness **C**reates **E**mpowerment. By facing your financial situation, including your needs and wants, you are becoming financially empowered on your *Unleashed* journey and that is something to celebrate. You are facing your finances!

Consider How They Grow

"The lilies say: Behold how we preach without words of purity."

CHRISTINA ROSETTI, ENGLISH POET

I am not one of those gardeners.

You know who I am talking about. One of those *otherworldly* people like my mother, who could spend hours in her flower beds with everything turning to vibrant colours and blooms at her touch with both delicate and astonishing fragrances. Starting in spring her gardens would overflow with lilies, morning glories, tulips, roses, clematis, mint, and so much more. Walking in her yard was like smelling the first gardens of the earth, maybe even Eden. I guess I can only imagine that place of complete intimacy with Creator God, but my mother's gardens would bring me there.

I know there is more to gardening than good luck or a green thumb. It takes planning, along with the right soil, the right amount of water, the right amount of sunlight, time, weeding, and lots of puttering. I spend enough time in my vegetable garden to know what it takes.

When I read Matthew 6, I hear a word of admonishment from the Master Gardener Himself about tending to the garden of our lives. It is a call to not worry, but instead to look at the beautiful lilies of the field as a means of helping us understand what a life free of worry can look like.

"So why do you worry about clothing? Consider the lilies of the field, how they grow: they neither toil nor spin; and yet..." (see Matthew 6:28-29).

And yet.

And yet, Solomon, the wisest, wealthiest king in ancient Israel, was not dressed in all of his glory like the lilies of the field.

"Have you ever considered how the lilies of the field grow?"
Do not worry.
"Take a closer look. Why are you worrying about what you wear?"
Do not worry.
"Take a look at the lilies."
Do not worry.

Apparently, lilies aren't fussy. They don't do well in copious amounts of water but, in all other respects, lilies are hardy plants. They can grow easily in a wide variety of soil with all kinds of pH levels. They grow well in full sun, partial sun, or light shade. You can plant them in spring or in fall. They also spread quite prolifically with care and tending; even without tending as is seen on the side roads of Eastern Ontario throughout the summer.

Why would Jesus direct us to the lilies when He talks about worry? Does considering the lilies combat the worry over food, clothing, and our other physical needs?

Consider. To consider something is to take the time to look, understand, and gain wisdom from it. When is the last time you stopped long enough to consider something—anything—nevermind the lilies? It takes time to consider. Are you taking the time to consider, to seek God, to talk to Him about what is troubling you?

Even as I write these words, I am praying and asking Abba Father to show me what He wants me to see as I consider His truth: Am I not of more value than the birds of the air and the flowers of the field? I am, and so are you.

Perhaps you have forgotten. That is why these words of Jesus are so important for today. It is time to remember: remember your worth, and step back into that Garden of Eden where you smelled the flowers, saw their beauty, and walked with God in the shade of the evening. He is waiting for you there.

MEDITATE: MATTHEW 6:25-32

CULTIVATING COMMUNION

Stop and take the time to consider nature. Go look at the birds, grass, and flowers. Sit and watch them. If it is winter when you are working through this book, discover a field, bush, or forest, and see how alive nature is even when covered in frost or snow. Sit or walk, but consider. Consider your value as a child of God. This is one of the steps that leads you away from worry to trust. Leave behind the worry of not having enough, and take the walk of trust in our tender, loving Abba Father. Listen to the old hymn, "I Come to the Garden Alone," and remember that you are His child and He knows your needs before you ask (see Matthew 6:32). Remember this exercise is a directive from Jesus Himself to stand against worrying about physical needs. Don't try to fight. Go into His presence and remember you are His.

> CONSIDER. TO CONSIDER SOMETHING IS TO TAKE THE TIME TO LOOK, AND UNDERSTAND, AND GAIN WISDOM FROM IT. WHEN IS THE LAST TIME YOU STOPPED LONG ENOUGH TO CONSIDER SOMETHING—ANYTHING—NEVERMIND THE LILIES? IT TAKES TIME TO CONSIDER. ARE YOU TAKING THE TIME TO CONSIDER, TO SEEK GOD, TO TALK TO HIM ABOUT WHAT IS TROUBLING YOU?

Clothed with Christ

"I delight greatly in the Lord; my soul rejoices in my God. For He has clothed me with garments of salvation and arrayed me in a robe of His righteousness, as a bridegroom adorns his head like a priest, and as a bride adorns herself with her jewels."

Isaiah 61:10 (NIV)

When I was a little girl, I loved to go shopping with my mom and sisters and get a new outfit at the mall. As I grew, I loved that time with them more and more. It's become an unspoken tradition of sorts. In fact, my sister just messaged me and invited me to shop with her on our next visit to Niagara. This experience growing up brought me a lot of joy for different reasons, but my favourite part was coming home and showing my Dad everything we had bought. I would steal away into a back bedroom and change into the pants and tops, skirts or dresses, and walk like a runway model into our living room. My Dad would look up from the baseball game and give me his attention, pouring out love, attention, and compliments. Christian authors John and Stasi Eldredge of Wild at Heart ministry would say that a very basic need inside of me was being met: I was being seen. In their book, *Captivating, Unveiling the Mystery of a Woman's Soul*, the Eldredges write, "We desire to possess a beauty that is worth pursuing, worth fighting for, a beauty that is core to who we truly are. We want beauty that can be seen; beauty that can be felt; beauty that affects others; a beauty all our own to unveil."[1] Reading about the lilies in Matthew 6 reminds me of the beauty that wants to be seen, pursued, and unveiled in all of creation. It reminds me that I have that same beauty, as well as that same desire to be seen. It also speaks to the places of my woundedness and worry, where I don't believe that God sees my beauty and I doubt His care. Today, my thirsty broken places listen as He speaks His truth again:

So why do you worry about clothing? Consider the lilies of the field, how they grow: they neither toil nor spin; and yet I say to you that even Solomon in all his glory was not arrayed like one of these. Now if God so clothes the grass of the field, which today is, and tomorrow is thrown into the oven, will He not much more clothe you, O you of little faith (Matthew 6:28-30, NKJV).

O you of little faith. Me of little faith. How much more will He clothe me, and love me, and care for me. Isaiah says that I am planted by God as a tree of righteousness for displaying His splendour and glory (see Isaiah 61:3). I am a beauty worth being cared for. I am seen by the One who made me. He doesn't forget and He doesn't leave. I am for His glory!

While I took great joy in shopping, having new clothes, and showing them to my earthly Dad, there is a deeper joy to be found in the truth of Christ's words and the Father's care. It is a truth that wants to penetrate beyond just the covering of outward flesh. God, as Jireh, is clothing us with His provision NOT ONLY for external material care, but for the deeper work of righteousness provided through Christ. He sees our worth and beauty and invites us into deeper trust. He beckons us, asking us to release worry and fear, offering His provision—the provision that arrays us in the Christ-clothes of righteousness.

God's word says that God clothes us, but not only that—He has provided us the Christ-clothes to wear. Isaiah 61:10 says, "I delight greatly in the Lord; my soul rejoices in my God. For he has clothed me with garments of salvation and arrayed me in a robe of his righteousness, as a bridegroom adorns his head like a priest, and as a bride adorns herself with her jewels" (NIV). The Message says it like this: "I will sing for joy in God, explode in praise from deep in my soul! He dressed me up in a suit of salvation, he outfitted me in a robe of righteousness, as a bridegroom who puts on a tuxedo and a bride a jeweled tiara. For as the earth bursts with spring wildflowers and as a garden cascades with blossoms, so the Master, God, brings righteousness into full bloom and puts praise on display before the nations."

I love how the Message says it as it draws me back to Matthew 6. If God so clothes the lilies of the field, how much more does He clothe us? And He doesn't just clothe us with clothes that are here today and gone tomorrow. He has clothed us with the righteousness of his Son — the costliest of garments because it cost His life. He has clothed us with white garments of redemption so that we can walk intimately with Him into eternity.

There is another thing about the clothing He provides. Not only is the garment of Christ our righteousness but it is the provision garment of love, acceptance, adoption, freedom, joy, hope, faith, forgiveness, favour, goodness, abundance, truth, resurrection life, Spirit-fruit, and so much more. It is the garment of our "enough-ness" where our poverty exchange is made, and we become enough in Christ, even more than enough. He exchanged His wealth for our poverty. He was stripped bare, bled in the flesh, and His skin was marred and torn and stained with blood. While he was publicly shamed in His nakedness, for the joy set before Him He endured the cross and scorned its shame and fulfilled His obedience (see Hebrews 12:2). He endured it, out of His love for His Father, and His love for us, so that we would not suffer in the shame of our naked fallenness any longer. He WANTED to clothe us in His righteousness.

This, then, is the way to walk. As God calls us to wake up and get dressed in Romans 13, let's rise and put on the trust, the confidence, and the beauty of the Christ-clothes of righteousness. In His clothes, we are prepared for every season. Let's not be luke-warm as the church of Laodicea written about in Revelation 3, but let's live a surrendered, intimate trust in Him that is passionate and filled with His beauty.

> THERE IS ANOTHER THING ABOUT THE CLOTHING HE PROVIDES. NOT ONLY IS THE GARMENT OF CHRIST OUR RIGHTEOUSNESS BUT IT IS THE PROVISION GARMENT OF LOVE, ACCEPTANCE, ADOPTION, FREEDOM, JOY, HOPE, FAITH, FORGIVENESS, FAVOUR, GOODNESS, ABUNDANCE, TRUTH, RESURRECTION LIFE, SPIRIT-FRUIT, AND SO MUCH MORE.

Jesus says, "You say, I am rich, have become wealthy, and have need of nothing—and do not know that you are wretched, miserable, poor, blind, and naked—I counsel you to buy from Me gold refined in the fire, that you may be rich; and white garments, that you may be clothed, that the shame of your nakedness may not be revealed; and anoint your eyes with eye salve, that you may see" (Revelation 3:17-18, NKJV).

This is Christ's invitation from lukewarm living to full-on trust in His love, His care, and His provision. God sees a beauty within us worth pursuing, and it is a beauty enhanced and redeemed by Jesus Himself. He clothes us in the righteousness of Christ, where He has given us beauty for ashes, the oil of joy for mourning, and a garment of praise for heaviness. We are the planting of the Lord for the display of His splendour and glory (see Isaiah 61:3).

MEDITATE: MATTHEW 6:28-30, ISAIAH 61:10, ISAIAH 61:3

CULTIVATING COMMUNION

Many years ago as a dear friend was praying for me, she saw this picture of me as a young child walking with God along the road. I was holding my Heavenly Father's hand and He asked me what I wanted. I told Him I wanted a brand new dress. In this vision, she heard Him say that He would take care of it, and I just needed to leave it with Him. Of course, the vision wasn't about a new dress, it was about so many practical and financial things I was worried about at the time. This picture of faith and intimacy has stayed with me for many years because it reminds me of the trust this younger version of myself had in her Daddy. I was willing to let go of my request and leave it with Him. I could have demanded how and when He was going to get me the dress, but I didn't. I just skipped off and entrusted this to His care.

As we consider His care, His practical provision in our financial journeys, but especially His spiritual provision for us through Jesus Christ, can you imagine yourself walking with your heavenly Father along the road, telling Him your needs and leaving your requests in His care? What does that look like? Throughout the day, as you remember your need and are tempted to ruminate in worry or the "lack" you are feeling in the moment, remember this picture. Bring your request to God again, release it into His hands, and then go back to what you were doing before worry crept in. Do this as often as you need to. Talk to God, release it into His care and walk back into your day knowing He sees you and provides for you with care.

My Shepherd Confirms His Care

Everyone has their concerns about finances; my husband Jerry and I were no exception. Jerry and I had no regular income, but depended on the gifts of supporters to do the work we were called to do in our ministry called *Adventures in Art and Music*. Together, we shared the gospel with families using his art and my music. We experienced both prosperous and lean times, but continued to trust the Lord to provide. However, one day a visiting friend made a comment on the state of our financial affairs saying, "If you don't make a change in the way you do things, you will be destitute in your old age!"

As I contemplated our friend's words, fear started to come to my mind and heart. That very same weekend, I received a miracle. In three different events, the song, "God will Take Care of You," was brought to my attention! I was visiting a friend and opened the hymn book to play a song, and the book opened up to, "God will Take Care of You." The next day, I attended a baby shower and before the party began, the hostess wanted us to listen to a contemporary version of, "God Will Take Care of You." Finally, on that Sunday, as my husband and I were getting ready to minister to a group of children, I glanced at the pulpit to see what the hymn selection was and (you guessed it) one of the hymns was, "God Will Take Care of You"!

What are the odds of this happening? It was my miracle, and it caused me to make a decision right there and then to never worry about my future. An interesting fact about this story is that this miracle was given to me, not to my husband. Jerry passed away at age 65 so he did not even experience old age. Our Father knows what we need.

BONNIE WALLACE
WINCHESTER, ONTARIO, 2021

More Than Enough

"You know the original meaning of that More Than Enough logo was all of that. The piece of our heart that is missing is held by God and only He can put that piece in. We try to fill that spot with all kinds of stuff, but nothing fits right. Only when God brings the piece—full of life—and fits it into place does He complete our puzzle.Essentially, it all makes sense once God brings the life piece."

DAVID VAN NOPPEN,
MTE OWNER AND FINANCIAL COACH

What are you worried about and what's behind the worry? Why is it such a struggle to trust God when His word is full of provision stories? Why do we worry when we see His faithfulness to us again and again?

We have already looked at our actual and perceived needs alongside Maslow's Hierarchy of Needs. Whether our worries come from the "extras" we want or from our struggle to provide basic needs like food, clothing, and shelter, many of us struggle on this trust journey with God.

Before we go any further, let's dig just a bit deeper into our cares and worries. Get out a piece of paper or your journal. Write down everything you can think of that worries you about money, banking, retirement, mortgages, provision, investments, loss of income, your children's post-secondary education, life insurance, or anything related to your finances.

Now, re-read your list and write down one sentence that summarizes all of these worries.

Write it here:

As I read this list of financial unknowns and worries the one thing I am realizing is:

_____

_____

_____

_____

There are as many endings to this sentence as there are people filling in this response. However, I would wager that many of your responses may share something in common. Does your one sentence of worry have anything to do with not having enough? Do you worry about not having enough money for food, water, clothing, vacations, retirement, bills, taxes, or for your children's education, either now or in the future?

We are worried that we simply won't have enough.

 It is interesting that at the naming of our financial coaching company, God spoke the words "More Than Enough" into former MTE owner Lynn Fraser's head, along with the logo of a puzzle with a missing puzzle piece. We have often talked with people about what that missing puzzle piece represents. For some, what's missing from their lives is the practical implementation of what we know as financial wisdom. At More Than Enough that is manifested through the coaching we offer, and how we encourage people to make practical steps to change their financial journeys into hope-filled, freedom stories. For others, the missing piece is the biblical understanding and foundation of what God wants us to know about financial stewardship.

When I see that puzzle, I see the missing piece of God's truth that He is my "More Than Enough." He is my guide and help. He is my portion. He is continually extending an invitation to me to look to Him

> WHEN I SEE THAT PUZZLE, I SEE THE MISSING PIECE OF GOD'S TRUTH THAT HE IS MY "MORE THAN ENOUGH." HE IS MY GUIDE AND HELP. HE IS MY PORTION. HE IS CONTINUALLY EXTENDING AN INVITATION TO ME TO LOOK TO HIM FOR DIRECTION.

for direction. He wants to help me understand the heart motivations behind my money decisions. He also wants to help me walk in fruitful, practical action steps that move me to a place of financial freedom. **He is the missing piece to my finances.** I love how David describes the missing puzzle piece. "You know the original meaning of that More Than Enough logo was all of that. The piece of our heart that is missing is held by God and only He can put that piece in. We try to fill that spot with all kinds of stuff, but nothing fits right. Only when God brings the piece—full of life—and fits it into place does He complete our puzzle. Essentially, it all makes sense once God brings the life piece."

There is a popular worship song by Elevation Worship and Maverick City called *Jireh*.[1] Many people have emailed me the link to the song over the past year, primarily because of the words *You are enough*.

Jireh You are enough
Jireh You are enough
I will be content in every circumstance
Jireh You are enough

In the YouTube video the vocalists repeat the phrase: "Forever enough. Always enough. Always more than enough." Always more than enough. He is my more than enough. I may struggle with bills, but He makes a way through the worry and the circumstances. It is His word to me, and I choose to believe it. As the song continues:

If He dresses the lilies with beauty and splendour
How much more will He clothe you
If He watches over every sparrow

How much more does He love you
More than you ask think or imagine
According to His power working in us
It's more than enough

Needless to say this has been a song I have put on repeat during this season of writing. As Hebrews 13:5-6 (NKJV) says, "Let your conduct be without covetousness; be content with such things as you have. For He Himself has said, 'I will never leave you nor forsake you.' So we may boldly say: 'The Lord is my helper; I will not fear, What can man do to me?'" He is my Helper. Even when I feel I do not *have* enough provision or money, I can *go to* my more than enough God to find what I need.

MEDITATE ON PHILIPPIANS 4:8-13

CULTIVATING COMMUNION
Change your thinking and what you are saying.

Instead of saying, "I can't afford it" or "I don't have any money," consider how you are thinking and speaking, and change it up: "We have money to spend, but we just haven't planned for that yet." Then make a plan to prepare for that expenditure. As David says, "Plan what you spend, and spend what you plan."

This is one simple shift that has immensely helped us in our own marriage and family. It also is a practical help that keeps us from worry, and helps us face the truth of where we are at. We actually have money. We have more than enough. We decide every day where that money goes. You may "feel" like you don't have money, but is that really true? Change your thinking and how you speak. So when your children ask if you can buy them that toy or book, you can simply say you need to talk about it together, and plan for it in your spending plan (budget). We love this because it also fights what some call the "poverty mentality" that says we don't have enough.

Remember contentment is possible because, as it says in Philippians 4:13, it's not about my ability to be content; it's about Christ's strength in me. Go re-read these Philippians verses and eat them. Jesus Christ is truly enough in you to strengthen you for contentment and trust.

Worry Weeds

"Any desire that drives us, controls our thinking, or preoccupies our minds can be a weed that hinders growth in our lives."

PAM DYCK, SOUL RESTORED

I think you can agree with me that God isn't vague about worry around money. He speaks clearly through His Son. It's His heart for us that we will keep turning to Him in our worry.

He knows that troubles—like worry—come to our lives, but He reminds us "to be of good cheer" for He (Jesus) has overcome the world. Cultivating trust and faith in Him is possible. He has overcome our worry about money, but as we will see in Mark 4, we need to do some weed pulling when it comes to worry.

My friend, Pastor Pam Dyck from Abbotsford, British Columbia, published her first book, *Soul Restored,* in the midst of the pandemic of 2020. In her book, she tells her redemptive story of freedom. It is an incredible story of strength, resilience, and God's love and hope. She speaks about her love of gardens, as well as her dislike of gardening. One day as she muttered about weed pulling, God reminded her that her life was like a garden that needed to be kept cleaned and cleared from the weeds of worry, unforgiveness, selfishness, anger, and negative thoughts.

She writes:

He reminded me that, like my life, I have to work everyday to keep myself "weed free" of negative thoughts...Those emotional and spiritual weeds are forever ready and willing to come in and take over the ground I've gained. Staying free takes work, and often in the past one of the biggest mistakes was thinking that once I'd done the work of forgiving or repenting, I shouldn't have to do it again. Wrong! Just like that garden box, I needed to stay on top of old habits and thought patterns that would try and overtake the good that God was doing in my life! I needed to keep my field cleaned and cleared.[1]

In the book of Mark, Jesus tells the story of the sower who sowed seed in all kinds of soil, and He speaks clearly of the weeds of the worries of the world that rise to choke out the good seed.

Pam continues,

In Mark chapter 4, Jesus warns of the choking influence of thorns. There are three kinds of pesky, prickly weeds that squeeze the life out of us.

The first weed Jesus warned of is the worries of the world, the anxieties of this age. Worry or anxiety means "to be drawn in different directions" or "to be distracted." We need to be aware of when we are getting distracted, and it usually happens when we get too busy.

The second weed Jesus spoke of is the deceitfulness of riches. Maybe you're thinking constantly about money, about not having enough or chasing more. Maybe you are in debt and yet you can't stop spending. That's a deceitfulness of riches that keeps saying you don't have enough and you need more! And you don't trust God to provide for you, so you keep providing for yourself while your debt mounts up.

The third weed that we find hindering fruitfulness in our lives is the desire for other things. Here we find the weed of a passionate desire or a craving. Some of these weeds are easily spotted, like sexual lust, an addiction to pornography, or perversions. But other cravings aren't so easily identifiable: food, clothing, jewelry, car, job, salary, a hobby or sport, or even the location or kind of house we live in. Any desire that drives us, controls our thinking, or pre-occupies our minds can be a weed that hinders growth in our lives.[2]

As you head into reading and meditating on the words of Christ, consider if there are any worries that are choking out the good that God is doing, and has done, in your life.

MEDITATE: MARK 4:1-20

CULTIVATING COMMUNION

Today, our time of communing with God involves something Pam asks us to do in her book:

One good way to spot if you've allowed some weeds to overtake your life is to check your conversations: What are you excited about? What do you talk with others about? What preoccupies your thoughts daily? Is it something honorable?[3]

This exercise Pam suggests may happen throughout your day or your week. You can journal about it or just talk to God. This will raise awareness in you about your worries, your thoughts, and how you are trusting God. Remember, "any desire that drives us, controls our thinking, or preoccupies our minds can be a weed that hinders growth in our lives."[4]

Here is a prayer Pam leaves us with:
Lord thank you for making me strong and brave. Help me to see myself the way you see me. Help me to see how far I've come, and not worry about how far I think I still need to go! Lord I recognize that just having one weed, one offense, growing freely in my heart can result in a take-over or a crop failure. Help me Lord, not to get complacent about the things in my life that still need to be taken care of. Help me Lord to stay vigilant about keeping my heart free from the lies of the enemy—those lies that try to tell me "this one little thing" is not that big a deal. Help me to desire to be free more

than I desire to hide or be comfortable. Help to identify the lies I've been believing and basing my life on, and to be ruthless in ridding myself of those lies![5]

Today Has Enough Trouble of Its Own

"God is a God of the present and reveals to those who are willing to listen carefully to the moment in which they live the steps they are to take toward the future."

HENRI J.M. NOUWEN, AUTHOR AND THEOLOGIAN,
FROM *IN THE NAME OF JESUS—REFLECTIONS ON CHRISTIAN LEADERSHIP*

Jesus said we shouldn't worry about tomorrow. He said worrying wouldn't add an inch to our stature or our lives. He spoke those words out loud to His disciples over two thousand years ago, and He says it to us today. He said don't worry because today has enough trouble of its own.

It wasn't until I read a teaching by Henri J.M. Nouwen, a Dutch Catholic priest, professor, writer, and theologian, that these words of Jesus came into my life and gave me a new perspective—a transformational renewing-of-my-mind moment.

I also came to see that I should not worry about tomorrow, next week, next year, or the next century. The more willing I was to look honestly at what I was thinking and saying and doing now, the more easily I would come into touch with the movement of God's Spirit in me, leading me to the future. God is a God of the present and reveals to those who are willing to listen carefully to the moment in which they live the steps they are to take toward the future. "Do not worry about tomorrow," Jesus says. "Tomorrow will take care of itself. Each day has enough trouble of its own" (Matthew 6:34).[1]

Why was this so profound for me?

It has shown me that if I could just live in each moment with God, doing and being all that He is saying and revealing—if I could just obey in each moment—**all that I need for tomorrow's uncertainties would come from today's moments.** Not only is this true for character qualities like how I can love, be still, and show patience, but also for how I live out my financial journey.

> IT HAS SHOWN ME THAT IF I COULD JUST LIVE IN EACH MOMENT WITH GOD, DOING AND BEING ALL THAT HE IS SAYING AND REVEALING—IF I COULD JUST OBEY IN EACH MOMENT—**ALL THAT I NEED FOR TOMORROW'S UNCERTAINTIES WOULD COME FROM TODAY'S MOMENTS.**

In practical terms, this means asking for God's guidance today in how to take care of what He has given me. This might involve:

- Talking to God about my finances.
- Talking about money with my best friend or partner for the first time.
- Looking at my monthly expenses and revenue to determine whether I live on less than I make.
- Paying an extra $20 on my credit card debt and making that a weekly automatic payment.
- Writing down 10 things I am thankful for today, instead of grumbling about what I don't have.

I think you understand. All of these steps you and I take today in our finances will pave a way for a future of positive cash flow management, less worry about money, and more trust in God, His care, and the abilities He has given you and me to take care of what He has given us.

MEDITATE: MATTHEW 6:34, ISAIAH 55:2

CULTIVATING COMMUNION

Live in the moment with God and ask Him what is the one thing you can do today toward your financial freedom. Write it down and then do that thing. It may look like praying over your finances. It may mean calling your financial coach to share some struggles. It may mean putting more money towards your debt. Or it may mean buying groceries for your neighbour. God only knows what He has for you today. Ask and listen, then carry it out.

In the next chapter, as we travel the road of cultivating trust, you will read a story about living in the way we have learned about today. Monica Froese lost her husband of 25 years, and God taught her to trust one moment at a time.

Living in Each Moment:
A Story of Encouragement

"Living in the moment each day has really strengthened me spiritually because it has taught me to trust God every moment for every little thing."

MONICA FROESE, *TENDER FRUIT GROWER*

My sister-in-law Monica Froese lost her husband Jamie in 2002. This is part of her story and how she listened to the Lord daily for instructions. It helped her through a very difficult time. It is the same help and hope available to each of us today.

Monica was married to Jamie for 25 years when a vehicle accident took his life. It was March 5, 2002. As a farmer, he had been waiting for specific cold temperatures necessary to harvest the last of his ice wine grapes. It was a long wait and a long harvest. The temperatures had not been cooperating, but, that wintry morning, the wait was over. I am sure my brother was looking forward to the end of this uncertain and weather-dependent harvest. I am also sure he was looking forward to the return of Monica and his three children from the Florida holiday they had planned together—a holiday he would otherwise have taken with them.

The accident happened before 10 in the morning. Monica and their children were in an American airport waiting on a connecting flight when they heard the news. Even writing these words, I am remembering the devastation of those days.

These were the circumstances surrounding Monica's life going forward in 2002. She was heading into the busy spring season of preparing orchards and land for the coming summer and fall harvests. She had children in their teen years. It was hard. Monica was not involved in the finances, or the day-to-day operations of the farm, yet she was now the sole owner of a beautiful farm in the Niagara Peninsula—a farm that needed management and tending. There was assistance from other farmers and family members, but the help that truly rescued her and gave her strength during those days was from God. Daily, He was her refuge, her strength, and her comforting help (see Hebrews 4:16).

This is what she did to lean into her new life with God.

Every day, she was sensing God directing her to ask for one thing. God would direct her to the one task she needed to carry out that day. He would even direct her to the file folder with the paperwork needed just for that day. This was how she lived. Doing what was needed— one thing each day. That is how she walked into the future. That is how she could leave the future in God's hands. She was doing what was needed in each day's moments. God became her husband in very practical ways, strengthening her daily to make decisions for her farm and her family.

This is what she says about that time in her life:

Living in the moment each day has really strengthened me spiritually because it has taught me to trust God every moment for every little thing. To this day if I have an issue in my life or I am not sure how to deal with a situation, I go straight to God and tell Him my problem and ask for His help and, then, I give it to Him and let it go. He has never failed me when I do this and trust Him.

Also, by living in the moment each day, I have learned not to worry about tomorrow, but concentrate on today and to be thankful for the wisdom I get from God for that day.

I do a lot less worrying and stressing. I give all my fears to God and He takes care of them—if I have trusted Him with them. How many times does God remind us not to fear? Joshua 1:9 has comforted and strengthened me many times. It's my favourite verse. "Have I not commanded you? Be strong and be of good courage; do not be afraid, nor be dismayed, for the Lord your God is with you wherever you go" (NKJV).

MEDITATE: JOSHUA 1:1-9

CULTIVATING COMMUNION

Just as Joshua suffered the loss of Moses, Monica suffered the loss of Jamie. However, God has instructions both for Joshua and Monica. Joshua 1:2 (NKJV) says, "Moses My servant is dead. Now therefore, arise, go over this Jordan, you and all this people, to the land which I am giving to them—the children of Israel." Monica's instructions were different obviously, but the care God gave Joshua is the same care and love He gave my sister-in-law. This is the same care God has for you. Take a few moments to think of a loss you have experienced. It may be a person, a job, a career, a child, or a relationship. It may be now or in the past. Ask God to show you His care for you during that time. Write down or speak out a prayer of thanks to Him for His care and love.

For example:
1. **What loss have I experienced?** In 2018, we decided to put Serena in grade 1 at a local school. After years of homeschooling my children, this was hard for me. It was like I was losing something while starting a new season in my life that I didn't understand.
2. **How did God show His care?** God provided helpful staff at the school who understood where I was coming from. They communicated with me often about her progress. I realize, looking back, how important it was for me to know she was being looked after.
3. **Prayer of thanks:** Thank you, Father, for providing loving people to surround Serena at school. I realize today how

important this provision was in my life, and how this was often a comfort to me when I saw her struggling. Thank you so much for providing for our family in so many big and small ways.

Provision,
Even in the Winter

"Therefore I say to you, do not worry about your life, what you will eat or what you will drink; nor about your body, what you will put on. Is not life more than food and the body more than clothing?"

MATTHEW 6:25 (NKJV)

"Look at the birds of the air..."

MATTHEW 6:26 (NKJV)

I am taking Jesus' advice. Even as I sit here and reflect on God's care for me and how I am called to a deeper walk of trust and faith, I am stopping to consider. I want to get a better understanding of how God takes care of the birds of the air in all seasons of life, and thereby understand how He takes care of me.

Outside my window on this beautiful November day, I am listening to the birds enjoying the unusually warm weather. The female cardinal outside my window is chirping, along with the chickadees. It is so noisy for this time of year, but so exceptionally welcoming and uplifting. My door is open so I can take it all in. With so many birds living near us all year round, I am continually reminded to "look at the birds of the air, for they neither sow nor reap nor gather into barns," and to remember that Abba Father feeds them. If He feeds them, won't He take care of me by feeding me and clothing me?

Through these few days that we have been meditating on Matthew 6, I have become more aware of how so much in this passage points to trusting God's love in all seasons of life. We are not to serve money and possessions in this world, but to serve God alone. We are not to trust in our own abilities to accumulate wealth but put our hands in God's and follow where He leads, not just in the spring, summer, and fall seasons of our lives, but in the winter too. At our home, on 25 acres of woodland and bush, birds nest all year long. We don't feed them, but they find what they need from the berries, insects, bushes, and trees that surround us, even in winter. After spending my winter snowshoeing in the bush, I am amazed at how active and alive it is. The plants may be buried under snow and the trees may be sleeping, but the birds and the animals continue their cycle of life. It is a constantly changing environment, and as I consider this winter place and how God provides for the birds, I am aware that God provides for me even in winter.

David and I have had some interesting financial experiences over 30 years of marriage. For a season, we lived from our savings account, having no income for over a year. It was a training time of trust as our savings didn't stretch quite far enough. Those times were often like winter months: nothing to harvest from our own land or our own abilities. God had called us to wait on Him through the "winter." We prayed. We lamented. We asked questions. We did our best to trust and obey. One of the verses God gave us in that season was from Hebrews 11. Like Abraham, He was calling us out to a place we didn't really fully know or understand. David had been an automotive technician all of his working life, and now he was to be a financial coach? "By faith Abraham, when called to go to a place he would later receive as his inheritance, obeyed and went, even though he did not know where he was going" (Hebrews 11:8, NIV).

THROUGH THESE FEW DAYS THAT WE HAVE BEEN MEDITATING ON MATTHEW 6, I HAVE BECOME MORE AWARE OF HOW SO MUCH IN THIS PASSAGE POINTS TO TRUSTING GOD'S LOVE IN ALL SEASONS OF LIFE.

With all the unknowns, David took one step of obedience after another, knowing God's plan and love was greater than we understood.

In February 2008, he began More Than Enough Financial Coaching with Lynn Fraser. This was part of our inheritance. Today, we own and operate this financial company and continue to seek God for His direction. In so many ways, God truly has given us more than enough—even in the winter.

MEDITATE: HEBREWS 11:8-12

CULTIVATING COMMUNION
What about you? Have you had winter seasons where God was asking you to look at the birds of the air to consider how valuable you are? Have you had winter seasons where God has fed you—physically provided in ways that bordered on the miraculous? Write down three ways God has provided for you in difficult times. Speak out or write out prayers of praise for His faithfulness.

Perhaps you are currently in a winter season. Being in the midst of the global pandemic, perhaps the whole world feels like it's in winter. I cannot speak to your specific situation, but God can and wants to. As I write these very words, I am listening to the song "The Blessing," featuring Kari Jobe, Cody Carnes and Elevation Worship.[1] This version is an hour long. I am listening to this long version to allow the truth of God's Word to seep into me.

The Lord bless you and keep you
Make His face shine upon you and be gracious to you
The Lord turn His face toward you and give you peace
Amen
May His favor be upon you And a thousand generations
And your family and your children
And their children, and their children
May His presence go before you and behind you
And beside you, all around you
And within you, He is with you
In the morning, in the evening
In your coming and your going

In your weeping and rejoicing
He is for you

This song came out in March 2020, and the artists of many nations around the world created zoom recordings of this song throughout the pandemic year.[2] The words are based on Scriptures found in Numbers 6:22-27, Exodus 33:14, and Deuteronomy 28:6. Why did this song have such an impact and go so viral around the world? I believe it was a reminder to us, and continues to be, that we belong to God. In all the difficulties, challenges, victories, and joys, He is with us and loves us. We have needed this reminder in an unprecedented year of global health and economic challenges. This song calls us back to God and His truth, again and again. So in this winter season of your life, don't forget that you belong to God and He belongs to you. In your weeping and your rejoicing, He is for you.

Seek Him First

The most often quoted Bible verse of my life is Matthew 6:33: *Seek first the kingdom of God and his righteousness and all these things will be given to you as well* (NIV). It is a truth that keeps believers in Christ focused on the destination, rather than the journey. It is the verse that gives the runner strength to jump the final hurdle and make it to the finish line.

No truer is this than in my own finances. I have, since my first job, tithed. I do not have great wealth in my investments or in an abundant bank account, nor do I always have cash to spare. Trusting God on the journey brings profound satisfaction for me. I cannot outgive Him in time, talents, or treasures, and He always meets my every need. All I do is seek Him and His righteousness. I do this first, each day. God rewards my faithfulness with His faithfulness. I must never think that *"all these things"* are shiny trinkets; instead they are the life sustaining gifts of God. Many of the *"things"* God provides are not tangible. They are the unseen *"things"* that can only come from God Himself. Yes, they do include my basic human needs, but this is so I can give Him all the glory and praise He deserves through my life.

Some say it is easy to become dependent on yourself; my experience has been the exact opposite. It is far easier to look at the beauty of God, His son Jesus, and His Kingdom than to look to myself for provision. He is continually pulling the pieces together for me, whether they be the balance in my bank account or retirement fund, or providing some of the simple pleasures of food, clothes, and shelter. When I seek the righteousness of God, I find it. When I am in the righteousness of God, things are all right.

DAN MASSEY
ROCKPORT, ONTARIO, 2021

In Good Company

"Now when Jesus saw the crowds, he went up on a mountainside and sat down. His disciples came to him, and he began to teach them."

MATTHEW 5:1-2 (NIV)

Jesus said, "Blessed are those…" So begins the Sermon on the Mount in Matthew 5, continuing through chapters 6 and 7. Jesus saw the crowd, sat down and began to teach. I just love the image that picture conjures up in my mind. He sits down and the people follow suit. He wasn't going anywhere, and neither were they. There were people to feed spiritually, emotionally, and relationally. His words were manna from heaven—He was manna from heaven—and they were ready to eat. That day if you were in that crowd, you were keeping good company. I can imagine the heat, the melody of His voice carrying through the mountainside, and the truth and love that was piercing through spiritual walls, pain, and unbelief. It was a feast of love and truth in good company. Others just like you surrounded Jesus, hungry and thirsty for what they had been praying for throughout the generations—prayers that their Messiah would come. That day, they were living in the time of the fulfilled promise. What was that like?

"Don't store for yourselves treasures on earth where moth and rust destroy…"

"You cannot serve two masters…"

"Look at the birds of the sky…"

"How much more does the Father care for you, Oh you of little faith?"

Words that were trustworthy came pouring out of the mouth of the

One who was the first from the beginning. They still come pouring out today, and if you position yourself to listen, you are in good company alongside others who are seeking, asking, and knocking. You are in good company with those who are cultivating trust, along with faith, hope, and love. As it says in Psalm 1, "Blessed is the man who walks not in the counsel of the wicked, nor stands in the way of sinners, nor sits in the seat of scoffers; but his delight is in the law of the Lord, and on his law he meditates day and night" (Psalm 1:1-2, ESV).

Blessed are they and blessed are you.

When you choose good company; when you choose His presence; when you choose His way; and when you delight in Him and His Word, you are giving yourself a good footing in your journey out of worry and anxiety to find the hope and freedom God promises. That day on the mountainside, people chose to be with Jesus. We have the same choice today. I have the same choice and, as much as I am able, I choose to come and sit on the mountainside of His Presence; to know His love, to bring my worries, and to hear His words of life and love that equip me for the challenges ahead. I choose to love as Jesus loves, give as He gives, and trust as He trusts. I need to be in His company and the company of others who are seeking as I am.

Why is the company I keep so important? Because there are so many voices.

So.
Many.
Voices.

There are many voices that speak different words, offering everything but the truth of who I am, who we are, and who God is. I **need** to be in good company, and I **need** to position myself in good company. It doesn't happen by

> THERE ARE MANY VOICES THAT SPEAK DIFFERENT WORDS, OFFERING EVERYTHING BUT THE TRUTH OF WHO I AM, WHO WE ARE, AND WHO GOD IS. I NEED TO BE IN GOOD COMPANY, AND I NEED TO POSITION MYSELF IN GOOD COMPANY. IT DOESN'T HAPPEN BY CHANCE.

chance. I intentionally seek to hear the words, and the voice of Jesus Christ every single day, hour by hour, minute by minute, all because there are voices that don't have God's best for me. Just as Jesus warned that we could not serve two masters, I need to understand what voices belong to the truth. Am I responding to the voice of mammon that draws me away from trust to the false promises of joy through the trappings of material possessions? Or am I responding to the voice of Christ inviting and drawing me further into His presence and into intimate relationship? Which voice of promise do I listen to?

These are choices I make daily—because they are daily choices. To walk out of worry and anxiety over my finances, I need to—I want to—choose Christ's voice daily. He is my answer. He has my answers. I don't always choose His voice. I know what it is to walk in the doubt of my failures, the accusations of the enemy in my ears, and how those voices ring louder than the truth of who I am.

As I write this, some of the words of a hymn and current worship song are seeping into my mind:

> *On Christ the solid rock I stand.*
> *All other ground is sinking sand…*
> *As He stands in victory*
> *Sin's curse has lost its grip on me*
> *For I am His and He is Mine*
> *Bought with the precious blood of Christ…*
> *He's a firm foundation…*
> *We don't have to understand to trust You, because our power comes*
> *from trusting not understanding.[1]*

We don't have to understand everything to put our trust in Him. Sometimes our financial journeys are filled with ups and downs, and we question His trustworthiness as Provider, as Sustainer, and the loving God we hear about. Consequently, I have resolved these past few years to change how I think about God, my Provision, and how He answers me. I have resolved that I do not need to have it all figured out. I don't need to have the explanations or have all my questions answered to trust Him and to love Him. This can feel uncertain sometimes, but my relationship is now filled with more wonder and mystery. Funny thing is, the more I have let go of trying to understand Him and how He works, the more I see of Him, hear from Him, and rest in Him. I am content to rest in the unanswered questions because I am discovering that He is who He says He is in the mystery of everyday living. It is marvellous and so is He. In the midst of this mystery of God, I commit to trust, for I know there is a well under my feet. It is a well of life that is His fulfillment of promise. He is the Lord. He never leaves and His river of life is flowing through me. However, if I am not drinking and eating from His well and His table, if I am not keeping good company with Him and others who seek Him, I can easily lose my way.

MEDITATE: MATTHEW 5:1-2

CULTIVATING COMMUNION

Today I invite you to think about the company you keep, and the voices you are listening to. On a piece of paper write a list of all the voices you hear in your day. Mine would include David, Hope, Justus, Serena, Holy Spirit, podcasts, movies, social media, books, friends, family. You get the idea. Then, next to each name/category write down how much time each day you spend listening to these voices. Next, answer the following questions:

1. Whose voices are speaking the most often or demanding the most attention? Circle your top three voices.
2. What is the loudest message in your life each day?
3. What nourishment are these voices giving you spiritually?
4. How are these voices encouraging you to cultivate trust with the Lord?
5. If you have the time, look at some of the voices again and write down what messages you are hearing from them on a regular basis.

After completing this exercise, and in light of your love and commitment to God, are there any changes that you would like to make so that you can be in good company with Jesus and other followers of Christ? Write down your thoughts.

You Cannot Serve Two Masters

"As for me and my household, we will serve the Lord."

JOSHUA, LEADER OF ISRAEL

Have you ever tried to serve two different people with two different objectives or agendas? If you have, then you know how challenging, if not impossible, it is.

When I was growing up and working on our family fruit farm in Niagara-on-the-Lake, I would spend my days in the fields or in the barns preparing for the fruit season. As a teenager, I had three bosses—my dad Jake, and my two brothers, Dave and Jamie. While they did share the same end goal of preparing for harvest and bringing in high yields, their methods differed. At the beginning of the day, Dave would send me out to do a job. A few hours later, Jamie would intervene and redirect me or tell me to do it a different way. This didn't happen every day, but when it did it was frustrating. They just weren't communicating with each other, and if they were, they sometimes disagreed. I got the brunt of that disagreement some days and I wouldn't know who to listen to.

Jesus tells us in Matthew 6 that we cannot serve two masters. In this context He is telling us we cannot serve God and mammon at the same time, "for either he will hate the one and love the other, or else he will be loyal to the one and despise the other" (see Matthew 6:24, NKJV).

Two of my friends crafted an eye-opening booklet around this very topic called *It's Not About the Money: Unmasking Mammon.*[1] Rev. Ray Borg and Jan Kupecz describe how every day we choose to live with either an earthly viewpoint for life, or one with eternity in view. We choose to serve God or we choose mammon.*

Here is what they say about mammon:

> Jesus personifies mammon and even gives it the status of a false god, an idol. He goes further to deliver an all or nothing claim that we cannot worship both. We must choose.
>
> These verses suggest there is a conflict or battle between two "masters." What exactly does that mean? In dictionaries, the word "mammon" is generally understood to be "wealth, possessions and may relate to "that in which one trusts" or in other words "an evil master that enslaves" or "any entity that promises wealth."
>
> Another definition is this—"wealth regarded as an evil influence or false object of worship and devotion."
>
> "Mammon" is the Aramaic translation for money. It was also thought to be the name of the ancient Syrian god of riches. Perhaps Jesus was doing more than just personifying mammon—perhaps as some scholars suggest, Jesus was referring to an entity.[2]

Mammon—whether a spirit, entity, or simply money and possessions—is used by the enemy of God to lie to us. As Rev. Borg and Kupecz suggest, "The spirit of mammon is pervasive and yet subtle, and it can be difficult to detect unless we remain vigilant against it. This spirit tries to persuade us to trust money more than we trust God."[3]

If we fail to make a choice to serve God EVERY DAY, we will choose mammon by default. As a financial coach, my husband David says that if we aren't intentional in our practical financial decisions, we will always default to debt. Since we live in a North American debt culture—no longer a culture known for saving money—we will often go to debt consolidation or enlarging our credit lines to accommodate more debt. Is this serving God? Or is this serving mammon?

We started this journey by looking at the whole topic of worry. Jesus tells us not to worry, and He also tells us to choose our master. I believe choosing to serve God daily, as imperfectly as I do that, is an antidote to worry. He is my choice every day and, no matter how I fail, I keep turning back to Him. That is serving God. We won't do it perfectly but we keep turning to Him both in the shame and in the victories, in the worries and in the trust. He—not the worry, or shame, or failure—becomes our focus.

Those summers on the farm were wonderful as I worked with my family to bring in the harvest. Even though the communication between my bosses got a bit mixed up sometimes, they shared the same goals and objectives. Not so the relationship between God and mammon: two different masters of two different kingdoms. God brings life. Mammon seeks to destroy our trust and intimacy with God. One leads to life; the other to death.

We can hear those words that Joshua once spoke to the children of Israel echo down to us today. "Now fear the Lord and serve him with all faithfulness. Throw away the gods your ancestors worshiped beyond the Euphrates River and in Egypt, and serve the Lord. But if serving the Lord seems undesirable to you, then choose for yourselves this day whom you will serve, whether the gods your ancestors served beyond the Euphrates, or the gods of the Amorites, in whose land you are living. But, as for me and my household, we will serve the Lord" (Joshua 24:14-15, NIV).

MEDITATE: MATTHEW 6:24, JOSHUA 24:14,15

CULTIVATING COMMUNION
Today we want to consider again the words from Scripture, alongside Brian Doerksen's song "Today I Choose to Follow You." https://www.

youtube.com/watch?v=ANAOg1rnTAo&ab_channel=bbacle

Today, choose again whom you will serve. If you choose to follow God, consider whether your life, commitment, and even your financial purchases reflect your commitment to God as Lord of your life. I have included a prayer here that may help you start talking to God about this important decision.

> Dear Abba Father,
> Today I choose You. To love, honour, and serve You. Just as Joshua declared so long ago, so I declare today: As for me and my house, we will serve You. I repent of serving mammon in my life. I know there are places I don't even see mammon's influence over me or my family. Open my eyes to see and my ears to hear, so that I become more and more discerning of who and what is influencing me. Today, I want to trust You over the world's financial systems. I want to trust You more than my bank account, my credit cards, and my own financial wisdom. Thank you for your forgiveness. Today I receive your forgiveness, your love, and your direction in my life. Lord, help me remember. Help me commit daily to You and Your ways.

(Note: You will find further study and information on the beautiful gifts of confession, repentance, and forgiveness at the end of this book.)

*To download a free copy of this booklet go to www.notmine. ca. Read this teaching and work through the questions and prompts provided. It is a book about discipleship and moving from "knowing" the words of Christ to implementing them. As A.W. Tozer said, "We can know the right words yet never be changed. This is the difference between information and transformation."[4]

The Key

"Seek first the Kingdom of God and His righteousness, and all these things shall be added to you."

Matthew 6:32 (NKJV)

"Then you will call upon Me and go and pray to Me, and I will listen to you. And you will seek Me and find Me, when you search for Me with all your heart. I will be found by you, says the Lord, and I will bring you back from your captivity; I will gather you from all the nations and from all the places where I have driven you, says the Lord, and I will bring you to the place from which I cause you to be carried away captive."

Jeremiah 29:12-14 (NKJV)

This is the Word of the Lord.

In some religious traditions, pastors or priests make this statement: "The Word of the Lord" after the public reading of God's Word. Today, as I read these verses from Matthew and Jeremiah, I am hearing these simple, holy words and remembering these holy moments with God as He reaches into my life to remind me, He will be found by me when I seek Him with all my heart. They are holy, sacred words that are true and powerful.

The Word of the Lord.

When I worry and fear about our financial situation or our financial future, I lose focus. I forget the Word of the Lord. I lose focus when I set my sights on what the world says is valuable—the trips, the home, the new cars, the retirement funds—and, in my worry, I wonder what I am seeking. Even though Jesus clearly tells us in Matthew 6 to seek

God's Kingdom first, what exactly does that mean? What does that look like?

The Kingdom of God is like.

So often Jesus spoke in parables of what the Kingdom of God is like: a pearl, a mustard seed, a narrow way. There is much mystery to me about what the Kingdom of God is really like because of the vast array of words and pictures Jesus uses to describe it. Honestly, I am glad it is a mystery. That's what keeps me seeking.

- Romans 14:17 says that the Kingdom of God is righteousness, peace, and joy in the Holy Spirit.
- Seeking the Kingdom first is to love the Lord my God, with all my heart, and with all my soul, and with all my mind and strength (see Deuteronomy 6:4-7).
- The Kingdom of God is loving others as I would love myself (see Matthew 22:37-40).
- The Kingdom of God is within me and within you as followers of Christ (see Luke 17:21).
- Within the Kingdom of God, the first shall be last and the last first (see Matthew 20:20-28).
- To seek God's Kingdom first is to give allegiance to Jesus, the King of this Kingdom. As Colossians 1:13 says, "He has delivered us from the power of darkness and conveyed (transferred) us into the kingdom of the Son of His love."
- His Kingdom is life, love, power, mercy, grace, and truth and out of it flows the fruit of the Spirit—love, joy, peace, patience, kindness, goodness, gentleness, and self-control (see Galatians 5:22-23).

The Kingdom of God is like.

Jesus continually invites us to come and see what His Kingdom is like. His word to us is that He will be found by us when we seek Him with all of our hearts. He will listen to us and we will be found. He will bring us back from captivity—from serving mammon, from serving self. He will gather us. He will gather us to Himself. And when we seek His Kingdom first, all the clothes, all the water, all the food will be provided for us. "For your heavenly Father knows that you need all these things" (Matthew 6:32, NKJV).

The Word of the Lord.

MEDITATE: MATTHEW 6:30-34, JEREMIAH 29:12-14, MATTHEW 27:37-40

CULTIVATING COMMUNION
How do we seek God's Kingdom? Jesus told us in Matthew 27 what the greatest commandments are: love God and love others. (Yes, that includes our "enemies.") This is one of many ways to seek God and His Kingdom first—love Him and others. So ask yourself, what is one thing you can do today or tomorrow that would be putting God and others first? Then complete that action.

Another idea: Why don't you sit down with your family and write some ideas together about what it would look like for you and your family to seek God's Kingdom in your lives. Write down your ideas and some ways you can carry them out. Share your ideas with a friend to help keep you accountable.

Remember: Seeking God's Kingdom first is a directive from Jesus; it is not optional for His followers. If you are transferred into His Kingdom, you do it His way. Jesus has told us these things because it is the good way—the best way—to live. It also takes intention, focus, and commitment. We do this one day at a time, with Jesus in every moment. As we grow in this way of living, our focus on Him will be stronger, and our worry less.

Seeking

"We don't have to wait until some future time, or even after
our bodily death, to access God's presence and the gifts He
possesses. Jesus' point is that having the treasure of God is far
more valuable in this life than any treasure the world might offer."

SKYE JETHANI, PASTOR AND AUTHOR

Seeking the Kingdom of God is one of the keys to cultivating trust and releasing worry in our lives. As we walk this journey, God wants us to gain more and more understanding of who He is, what His Kingdom is like and how He loves us, as a means of building trust in Him, not only in our finances but in other areas of our lives as well.

According to *Strong's Concordance,* the Greek word for seek in Matthew 6:33 means to seek a thing in order to find it.[1] We can do that by thinking, meditating, reasoning, and enquiring into it. We seek after the kingdom of heaven, aim for it, strive after it, and even crave it. The thing we seek becomes our desire.

Jesus had a lot to say about the Kingdom of God and the Kingdom of Heaven. From my limited half-century perspective, I know I need more than my one or two dimensional sight or thinking to understand the nuances of what He spoke—what it means to seek His Kingdom. As I have been learning from the Lord over the years, what my heart wants isn't always aligned with what He wants for me. Metaphorically speaking, it's like I need three-dimensional glasses or a Virtual Reality (VR) headset to fully engage in understanding all that Jesus said and lived. Then, I need to take what I see and hear and create habits that reinforce this Kingdom living.

SEEKING THE KINGDOM OF GOD IS ONE OF THE KEYS TO CULTIVATING TRUST AND RELEASING WORRY IN OUR LIVES.

Defining the Kingdom of God or Kingdom of Heaven is not black and white for me. In some places, these two terms are used interchangeably in Scripture.[2] Scholars have differing opinions on whether or not they are the same thing.[3] So as to keep it simple—because I like to keep it simple—let's use Jesus' life as the template for seeking God's Kingdom first. We can read what He said and we can watch how He lived. Here are three simple observations I make about how He lived.

1. Prayer and time with His Heavenly Father was the highest priority. He would often go off to be alone to pray, and His life flowed out of that relationship.
2. Doing God's will was another priority. From what we see and hear from Jesus, His Kingdom pursuit was doing the will of His Heavenly Father. Jesus told His disciples that His food was to do the will of the one who sent Him (see John 4:34). He lived out of that calling to the point that it nourished Him.
3. He gave and gave and gave. He gave of His wisdom, in His teaching, of His time, and out of His love. He healed, He created, and He spent time with the people God had given Him to lead and love. He did this out of His being—out of being God's Son.

Jesus said on many occasions that the Kingdom of God was near at hand (see Matthew 4:17 and Mark 1:15). The Kingdom was there in His lifetime, and it continues to be here today in ours. The Kingdom of God is not just about the life to come. His Kingdom is now among us, where God rules and evil is powerless.

Author, pastor, and scholar Skye Jethani writes in his devotional book, *What If Jesus Was Serious,* that the "kingdom of the heavens has broken into our world, and a new way of life is now possible. In the Sermon on the Mount, therefore, Jesus is unveiling a new ethic for those who belong to a new kind of kingdom that is not of this world."[4]

Jethani also says that laying up for ourselves treasures in heaven (see Matthew 6), in the context of the Sermon on the Mount, is not about a realm in the future.

> There are other passages of Scripture that speak of future blessings (like 1 Peter 1:4-5), but Jesus is speaking of something different here. He is talking about a treasure that is accessible to us right now, and this treasure is the presence of God in our lives. We don't have to wait until some future time, or even after our bodily death, to access God's presence and the gifts He possesses. Jesus' point is that having the treasure of God is far more valuable in this life than any treasure the world might offer.[5]

Wow! I think I need to read that again. God, the Creator who loves me, is accessible to me today because of Christ's death, resurrection, and life! He is my heavenly treasure and He is more valuable than any treasure this world offers!

MEDITATE: MATTHEW 14:22-23, JOHN 4:30-34, MARK 1:29-39

CULTIVATING COMMUNION

Are any of the three priorities of Christ, your priorities?
1. Do you take time to be alone with God?
2. Is obedience to God important to you? Do you follow through on what He says to you?
3. From those places of being and obeying, does giving of your time, talents, resources, and finances flow from your life?

Consider today's verses and spend some time thinking about the priorities of Christ. In his book *The Ruthless Elimination of Hurry: How to Stay Emotionally Healthy and Spiritually Alive in the Chaos of the Modern World*, pastor and author, John Mark Comer writes that to be a disciple or "apprentice" of Jesus means you need to be with Jesus, become like Him, and do what He would if He were you.[6] "If you want to experience the life of Jesus, you have to adopt the lifestyle of Jesus."[7] Cultivating trust in God means not only following the truth of Jesus Christ, but doing so His way. If I want the life of Jesus—a life of freedom, joy, love, trust, faithfulness, patience, and kindness in the midst of life's seasons—I need to adopt His lifestyle. Easier said than done, I realize, but there is always hope. He has given us His Word. He has given us His Spirit. He has given us His presence. He has given us His love. We are not without aid!

So let's go back to the three priorities of Jesus. Choose one of them to dig into this week by first reading about Jesus in the Gospels and, then, asking Him to help you live out what matters to Him.

Treasure Worth Seeking

"Don't give up, It's just the hurt that you hide.
When you're lost inside, I'll be there to find you.
Don't give up, because you want to burn bright.
If darkness blinds you, I will shine to guide you."

*ADAPTED FROM THE SONG "YOU ARE LOVED (DON'T GIVE UP)"
FROM JOSH GROBAN'S AWAKE ALBUM*

Mary lost her coin. David lost his sheep. They both searched and searched. They asked their neighbours. She swept and cleaned. He climbed the hills. Mary found the coin under the rug. David found the lamb tangled in the thicket. Both rejoiced at what they had found. What was lost was found, and what was thought dead was alive.

This is one of the roles of Jesus as Shepherd in His Kingdom. He is the One who seeks us out to bring us to Himself. He seeks and searches us out until we are found. We are of value and are treasures worth seeking. Scripture tells us that Jesus as Shepherd will leave the 99 to go and find the one (see Luke 15:1-7). He seeks us through rough terrain, crevices in the mountains, and under bushes covered with thorns. He doesn't stop looking. When He finds the one, He carries her back to the others, to the place of safety and provision.

Today, I am thinking about the tenacity with which Jesus comes looking for each of us. You know what it is like. When you have lost something precious to you, you search and search. You stay up late looking. Many years ago, my neighbour Joanne Doucet lost her wedding rings in the church parking area. She had been putting cream on her dry hands as she sat in the car. Without putting her rings back on her finger, she opened the car door and got out. The rings had been sitting in her lap. It was much later during the service that she looked down and realized her wedding rings were not there. They fell somewhere between her car and the church door. She searched. Her husband searched. Friends and family searched, but all came up empty-handed. I don't recall the entire sequence of events, but Joanne and her husband returned to the church many times to look, without success. The church lawn was mowed once if not twice during this time, and we all wondered if her rings would be found. Then one day, her husband and parents thought they would look once more. You see, Darlene McMillan, another friend from church, had had a dream. In the dream, she saw an angel reach into her pocket and take out the rings and place them carefully in the grass one on top of the other. I don't recall if Darlene told Joanne the dream before or after she found the rings but, nonetheless, they did find the rings in a little divet of dry ground, one on top of the other.

We all considered it a miracle, and we celebrated. In the light of the joy Joanne had experienced in finding something so precious, she baked pies for our 100-member congregation. We celebrated her joy, and it became our joy, and we had a feast. Those rings were significant to my friend, and in God's care for her, they were significant to Him.

In remembering this story, I am remembering the joy of that moment and the realization of how much God cares about each of us and the details of our lives. As Joanne searched for those rings, Jesus searched for me. He continues to call and search for those sheep who are wandering off. I am the significant treasure He looks for—and so are you. You are the significant treasure that is worth seeking and so are all people from every tribe, nation, and tongue. It is in His role as Shepherd-King that Jesus sacrificed His riches, His position, and His life, to seek and save us who are lost and wandering. He came to bring us back to life and to breathe into us again His purpose, love, fearlessness, and power. Not only did He seek us out by being born as a man over 2000 years ago, He came to offer His life. Dying for us and rising alive from that grave, Jesus made a way for us so that we could again receive the fullness of relationship with Himself, His Father, and His Spirit.

It is Jesus, this sacrificial Shepherd-King, who invites us to trust Him in the midst of life's circumstances and worries. He wants us to cultivate trust in Him, and we can do this as we understand we are loved by, and significant to, God. This is essential in our relationship with Him. If we can start to grasp this truth, we can start to trust Him with our lives and the lives of those we love. We can begin to release our worries about money because in the very heart of who we are, we know He cares. Scripture says simply in 1 Peter 5:7, "Cast all your anxiety on Him because He cares for you" (NIV). You are loved by the God who made you. The weight of the world may be pressing in on you but you are loved. Look up and see. He is the great Shepherd who leaves the 99 to go and find one. You are His treasure worth seeking.

MEDITATE: LUKE 15:1-10, EPHESIANS 3:14-21

CULTIVATING COMMUNION

There is a song that music artist Josh Groban recorded a number of years ago for his Awake album called "You are Loved (Don't Give Up)," written by Thomas Salter and Molly Kaye.[1] It spoke to me in a season of loss, rejection, and grief. I remember playing that song on repeat because I so needed God's truth rooting me. As I listen to it today, I am reminded of that season and the love God revealed.

Listen to the song, "You are Loved (Don't Give Up)." Then, take the Word of God and read the words from Luke 15:1-10 and Ephesians 3:14-21. Notice the response of the Shepherd and the woman in Luke 15.

- The Shepherd lays the lost sheep on His shoulders. Rejoicing.
- The woman, when she has found it, calls to her friends and neighbours, saying, "rejoice with me."

Have you ever lost something precious? Were you able to find it? Reflect on that time and how you responded. Did you search and search? Were you saddened by the loss? Now consider what Jesus feels towards the people He loves. Leave this time of reflection with a prayer of thanksgiving in your heart for the love He has just for you.

For example:

1. **Have you ever lost something or someone?** I had a misunderstanding with a friend and, for a season, I lost the friendship.

2. **How did that loss make you feel?** Terrible. Sad. I cried a lot. I questioned and blamed myself.

3. **Did you search for what you lost?** I prayed about how I could repair the broken relationship. At the time I did what I could, but I knew that God was asking me to wait. I guess I stopped searching for a while.

4. **How do you think Jesus felt about your loss?** I haven't really thought about that before. I guess, or, I think, He would be feeling sad too. But I also realize that He sees both sides like I can't. He told me to wait because of what He was working out in both of us. I understand that now.

5. **Did you ever find what you lost?** Months and months later, I met my friend again and we talked about what happened. We apologized and hugged each other and were restored in friendship.

6. **Prayer of thanks:** Dear Father, I am so thankful for this journey of friendship You allowed me to walk through. I learned to trust You—even when it hurt. I learned to wait. Not all my broken relationships have been restored in my life but this one was and I am so grateful to You for leading me through it. Thank You for being my loving Shepherd-King.

SIDE BAR:

Treasures Worth Seeking

THE HEAVENLY TREASURE OF CHRIST HIMSELF

Here's one more thought about laying up treasures in heaven. Skye Jethani, cohost of The Holy Post podcast, recently authored a devotional on the words of Christ found in Matthew 5, 6, and 7.[1] He asks the question in the title of His book, *What if Jesus Was Serious?*. What if Jesus was serious about all that He taught and revealed? This, of course, may sound to you like a rhetorical question. But the point of his book is to face whether or not we really believe and live like Jesus was serious about what He said. In other words, do we believe and live what *we say* we believe?

Jethani makes an interesting comment about laying up treasures in heaven, believing that Jesus isn't talking about the future heaven and a reward to come:

We assume what Jesus means is: rather than enjoying life now, serve God and His kingdom, and you'll really be well off in the age to come! This future orientation, however, is not present in Jesus' actual words. There is nothing in this portion of the Sermon on the Mount about a reward awaiting us after death, or about delaying one's gratification until Christ returns. These are ideas we've projected onto the text; they're not in the text itself.[2]

So, then, what is the treasure in heaven? The heavenly treasure is Christ Himself, according to Jethani. His presence. His goodness. Now. Not just in the future to come when we pass from this life to the next. If we want to find those promises and blessings of eternity with Christ, there are many we can find. We only have to go to 1 Peter 1:3-5, where we are told that we are begotten "again to a living hope through the resurrection of Jesus Christ from the dead, to an inheritance incorruptible and undefiled and that does not fade away, reserved in heaven for you" (NKJV).

Jethani's words about Matthew 6:19-21 did get me thinking, and reinforced my own belief that I seek God and His Kingdom for the reward of being in relationship with Him, the Creator and Lord of all. I seek treasure in Christ because He is my reward. For me, storing treasure in heaven is living today in, and for, God's glory, and for the good of others. That is His heart for me, and it is now treasure. It is partnering with God, and meeting Him in the places where He is loving people into His Kingdom. My reward is in the abiding place with Christ, where no rust or moth can destroy or eat away at my time spent with Him, or my worship of Him. In view of this treasure, I can daily reorientate my heart, my habits, and my worship to Him.

More Treasure Worth Seeking

"Do not lay up for yourselves treasures on earth, where moth and rust destroy and where thieves break in and steal; but lay up for yourselves treasures in heaven, where neither moth nor rust destroys and where thieves do not break in and steal. For where your treasure is, there your heart will be also."

MATTHEW 6:19 (NKJV)

In the previous chapter, we came to understand that Jesus searches for us—His precious treasure. Mary found her coin, David found his lost sheep, and Jesus found us. As we are found, we look to Him as our example of how to seek and find the treasures that matter most to Him. In Matthew 6, Jesus commands us as His followers to seek the treasures of the Kingdom. He tells us to seek the Kingdom of God first, and His righteousness—just as Mary sought the coin, just as David sought his lamb. Seeking His Kingdom and the treasures of His Kingdom involves focusing on what is of importance to Christ and His Kingdom.

So, where is my treasure? What is my heart set on? And what matters to the heart of God?

God has transferred us into the Kingdom of His Son (see Colossians 1:13). He asks us to seek His Kingdom first, loving Him with all of who we are and loving others as we love ourselves. He also asks us to focus on building treasure in heaven—not on earth—caring about what matters to Him.

But here's the thing: trying to deceive God just doesn't work—

transparency, honesty, and vulnerability are really our best options. Understand that, metaphorically speaking, God has a stethoscope in hand that is attuned to our hearts. He is not deceived. He knows what is going on and knows exactly what has our heart's attention. He knows better than we do.

In terms of finances, one simple way to check my heart is simply to look at my bank account. What matters to my heart will be reflected in the numbers—because the numbers don't lie.

So take a look and consider some of the following:

- What does my bank account activity say about what I am committed to?
- Is the money I am spending on extra-curricular activities, for instance, going towards others or only myself?
- What is my charitable giving like? I say that I like to give to others, but does my bank account reflect that value?
- Does the spending I see reflected in my bank account build the Kingdom of God?

Building treasure in heaven is yet another way of combating worry. How?

> IN TERMS OF FINANCES, ONE SIMPLE WAY TO CHECK MY HEART IS SIMPLY TO LOOK AT MY BANK ACCOUNT. WHAT MATTERS TO MY HEART WILL BE REFLECTED IN THE NUMBERS— BECAUSE THE NUMBERS DON'T LIE.

It puts value on things that can't be stolen so we won't be worrying about keeping our stuff safe and thief-proof. We start investing in time with Him—discovering, seeking, knocking. We start investing in people, relationships, businesses, families, and communities that God is asking us to pour into. Remember it is His: His people, His money, and His resources that He has given to us to manage. If I truly believe it is all His, then it is also His worry and His responsibility. So often I think I have some kind of control over my giving, my time, my resources. But in truth, a lot of my worry would disappear if I truly understood it is not mine. It is not about me. My money is His money; it is about furthering His Kingdom and purposes, not my own.

If I spend my time, money, resources, and talents on building and encouraging others, those gifts and resources cannot decay or be stolen. I may wrestle with how to invest in God's Kingdom and how to love others, but that wrestling is for eternal purposes, it is not worrying about attaining, keeping, or preserving something that I can't take with me to the grave or into eternity.

Mary lost her coin. David lost his sheep. They turned over everything and asked everyone to help them find what was most precious. Jesus has done this in the purest form. He has taught us what matters and how to seek after what cannot be stolen, burned, or destroyed.

MEDITATE MATTHEW 6:19-21, MARK 10:17-22, ROMANS 12:1,2

CULTIVATING COMMUNION

Imagine yourself as the rich young ruler from the reading today. How might he have felt after this intersection with Jesus? Note that before Jesus offered His challenge to the young ruler, Scripture says He looked at him and loved him. He loved him, and yet He still let him walk away.

Have you ever had a similar experience with the Lord as this rich young ruler had? What was your response? Perhaps the Lord is saying something to you today about some obstacles and heart treasures that don't align with His love and ways for you. If so, try the following exercise.

Hear the Lord speaking to you, and fill in the blank. In Matthew 19:21, Jesus says, "If you want to be perfect, go and _____, and you will have treasure in heaven; and come, follow Me." Is He showing you any obstacles? For the rich young ruler it was money and possessions. Is that an obstacle for you?

OR

Ask the Lord what it looks like for you to store up treasures in heaven. How can you start living out what He shows you? Whatever comes up for you today during this time, write a prayer of thanks for God's love and care for you, even as you discover these intimate parts of your journey with Him. You may want to read about repentance at the end of this book and take some time confessing and repenting about anything that has got in the way of your relationship with God. Remember, there is no shame in turning back to Him. Jesus has taken it all. He wants to encourage our growth. He wants to free us from what keeps our hearts hidden and enslaved. This is a daily journey of following Him. Take this time to thank Him for seeking, finding, and leading you.

From Financial Prison

to Financial Freedom

I remember a dark night in November 2017. I was married with five young children. I pondered my current life situation: marriage on the verge of separation, illness in the family, mental, physical, and emotional burn-out, and deep financial debt as I lived continually in the negative, from paycheque to paycheque.

What would happen to me if I lost my marriage, my house, my work? What if I lost my health and was unable to care for my children? Anger, shame, fear, and hopelessness gripped my heart.

It was then I heard a still voice whisper in my heart: "If you lost everything, you still have me! I will never leave you, nor forsake you!" I recognized the voice of my Savior, Jesus. In that moment, light shined in my heart and hope sneaked in. I will live the abundant life that Jesus promises to those who belong to him.

In the months that followed, my marriage fell apart and I was separated. I had a small car that could not fit my whole family. I owed tens of thousands of dollars to the Canada Revenue Agency (CRA), as well as on my car loan, credit card loans, and my mortgage. I was self employed, without benefits.

Romans 8:28 says, "And we know that in all things God works for the good of those who love him, who have been called according to His purpose."

In that season, I started to experience the support of the community of family, friends, and believers the Lord had given me. I was provided generously with a financial coach at More Than Enough as well as a small accountability group called *Unleashed*. My trust in my own performance for financial freedom was exposed. My "fear of lack"—that often guided my financial decisions—was also revealed. Laying down my mask, I opened my financial books and accepted the truth that I needed to be vulnerable with my coach, Sarah-Jane, and my small accountability

group. Instead of judgment and condemnation, I received grace, compassion, and support in prayer.

Our matrimonial home was sold, and I moved in with my parents. The Lord provided a car that I could purchase for cash, and my car loan was paid off. Steady payments were made to CRA, credit cards, and family, and friends. My debts were being paid off one by one. In all of this, I learned to be content with the provision of my heavenly Father.

Nine months later, Covid-19 began and my income dropped to almost nothing. Once again, my heavenly Father manifested Himself as the Good Shepherd. He provided for our needs regardless of my ability to work outside the home. I learned to trust the Lord in making difficult decisions that needed to be made, in preparation for the future.

Now, when I am discouraged, the testimony of my *Unleashed* small group and my community keeps me moving forward as I hear their money stories and how the Lord has brought them freedom. I am learning to trust in God's love. I am His beloved daughter. I am redeemed by the precious blood of Jesus, from all my money mistakes and I am called according to His own purpose.

Now, I am no longer living from paycheque to paycheque. Instead, I am currently learning to steward the resources allocated to me. I am learning to be grateful and satisfied with what I have, and I am learning to give and to invest wisely. I am learning to remain connected to the Vine of Christ, to ask, and to wait for His guidance and His provision.

"You open Your hand and satisfy the desire of every living thing" (Psalm 145:16, NIV). This is what my Abba has done for me.

MARTINE PIERRE-LOUIS
OTTAWA, ONTARIO, 2021

Throwing Glitter

"When we operate out of abundance, it's easy to throw glitter...
When we operate out of scarcity, it is easy to lint pick."[1]

BLOGGER ASHLEE GADD

We just celebrated our daughter's first double-digit birthday. Serena turned 10 on May 25th, and from where I sit this morning, I am surrounded by glittery banners, birthday hats, and banners. If you came to have a coffee-visit, I am sure you'd know what's been going on: we've been celebrating!

These celebrations for our daughter were all about throwing glitter—if not literally—then metaphorically. This was her second Covid-lockdown birthday. That meant no celebrations in-person with her young friends. That meant family only, and on this special birthday we wanted to make an extra effort to throw as much metaphorical glitter on her as we could, especially because of the isolation she's been in. One way we did that was to pour words of encouragement and appreciation all over her. We spent time telling her we love her and what we love about her. We do this kind of thing at all our family birthdays. It is an opportunity to express our love and appreciation and our way of throwing life and encouragement into each other's lives.

I hadn't thought about my love for glitter throwing until my friend, Tanya, used those words to describe me. Borrowing words from blog writer Ashlee Gadd, she called me her "glitter throwing friend."[2] I love to celebrate. I love to celebrate people and milestones and any joys I see others experiencing. I love parties, laughter, and living large. Living small and hidden away serves no one, in my opinion. I take great delight in hot coffee or cold coffee. Not lukewarm. I am all in or not at all. I love to give—and sometimes extravagantly. Frugality and "shopping the sales" don't serve my personality well—although it sometimes serves my bank account very well. I love to encourage people and tell them the beauty of how they were created. I get excited over the smallest of victories and cry over the smallest and hardest fought battles. I like to throw glitter: as 1 Timothy 6:17 states, God has given us all things to enjoy—and I do my best to enjoy all of them!

> LIVING SMALL AND HIDDEN AWAY SERVES NO ONE, IN MY OPINION. I TAKE GREAT DELIGHT IN HOT COFFEE OR COLD COFFEE. NOT LUKEWARM. I AM ALL IN OR NOT AT ALL. I LOVE TO GIVE— AND SOMETIMES EXTRAVAGANTLY.

I don't want you to get the wrong idea. I am not always throwing glitter. Sometimes, I am negative and complain-y. I have taken a glitter-throwing hit with all the Covid-19 lockdowns during the global pandemic—living through unexplained fatigue, stress, and bouts of anxiety. Sometimes, I drink lukewarm coffee. I struggle with selfish habits. I continue to learn the kindergarten lesson of sharing, and I don't always like it. Some days people bug me, and I don't have a lot of nice things to say.

And the verses in Matthew 6 about moths and rust are sometimes a wrestle for me. If I am being honest, I struggle more than sometimes. Just as I like to celebrate and live large, I like the "things" of the world as part of that glitter throwing and, in my heart, I know they can become idols that steal from my relationship with Jesus. While the celebrating and glitter throwing is what I love and part of how I am wired, I know there is a fine line in my heart where I can cross over into loving the gifts more than the Giver.

"Do not lay up for yourselves treasures on earth, where moth and rust destroy and where thieves break in and steal, but lay up for yourselves treasures in heaven, where neither moth nor rust destroys and where thieves do not break in and steal. For where your treasure is, there your heart will be also" (Matthew 6:19-21, ESV).

For where my treasure is, there you find my heart.

I don't know about you, but sometimes I just love the beautiful things of this world. I love jewelry. I love books. I love a good cup of coffee. I love southern beach vacations. I love "ease." I love "comfort." I love the finer things in life, and I try to figure out a way to gain all of it. Sometimes, I spend too much time thinking about all of it. When I am all in I am all in, and these things of the world start sitting on the throne of my heart as if they can bring me some kind of happiness.

I believe God has made me to be His glitter-throwing girl. He has made me alive and abundant. But sometimes, the desire for those God-given gifts becomes an obstacle to loving God and others. I start relying on the gifts to bring joy instead of on God Himself. The red flag starts waving when I get honest and realize how much time I spend thinking about, or meditating on, those gifts, and how to attain those things, while neglecting to talk to God about them. If I hide a purchase from David, that is a sure sign something has gone wrong.

Sometimes I gather the courage to ask myself a hard question: Am I losing sight of the Kingdom of God as I pursue the glitter of the world? The answer is sometimes "yes."

Abba God speaks to us about such loves. I John 2:15-17 says, "Do not love the world or anything in the world. If anyone loves the world, love for the Father is not in them. For everything in the world—the lust of the flesh, the lust of the eyes, and the pride of life—comes not from the Father but from the world. The world and its desires pass away, but whoever does the will of God lives forever" (NIV).

These words are no joke and, if I let them, they penetrate through the onion layers of my heart.
"Oh God help me to love You more—love You most. Blessed be the God and Father of our Lord Jesus Christ who remembers we are dust, whose mercies are new every morning, and who makes a way for me in all of this."

I want to set my heart, my mind and my habits, on things above. I want to focus on His Presence, His love, His goodness, as I walk on the ocean waves of life's unrelenting and changing circumstances. Less of what I want and more of what He wants. Or again, if I'm honest, I want to want what He wants more than what I want. When I ask for more of Him in my life, I know that means less of me as I align myself with what matters to Him. The Psalmist in Psalm 37:4 says, "He will give us the desires of our hearts, when we take delight in Him." As I delight in God, His desires become mine.

Today, I want to take delight in Him more than I delight in earthly wealth, possessions, or accolades. Today I am also reminded that throwing glitter is how I am wired, and I know that throwing glitter on Serena this weekend was good. Celebrating others and throwing glitter is part of His abundant life poured through me. It's how I am made and it is good.

God is an abundant provider. He is not a miserly giver. Ecclesiastes is filled with commands to enjoy what He has given us. So as we consider—as I consider—what loving the world looks like in my life and what loving Him looks like, I am reminded that He is not set on restraining me, but setting me free to throw His glitter into, and over, others. I want to do this by storing up treasure in Him. Will you join me?

MEDITATE: PSALM 37:1-7

CULTIVATING COMMUNION
Take delight in Him. What does that look like for you today?

Choose a quality trait about God that you love. You can start with the list below if that will help.[3] Then take that truth about God into your day, as you walk, as you journal, and as you set your eyes on Him. Find the Scriptures that declare who He is. Thank Him for who He is. This is a beautiful practise that helps us train our minds on Him. This alignment will take our eyes off the world and set them squarely on the presence of Himself and His Kingdom in our lives. Thoughts of Him will also replace the worry that is knocking at the door. So take delight in Him and He will grant you the desires of your heart. For, in this place, your heart will grow to desire what His heart desires.

Among so many other qualities, God is:

Good	Changeless	True
Powerful	Almighty	Pure
Great	Glorious	Faithful
Excellent	Righteous	Radiant
Full of Love	Just	Magnificent
Wise	Full of Grace	Worthy
Holy	Sinless	All-Sufficient
Merciful	All-Knowing	Light of the World

Good Eyes Filled with Light

"The eye is the lamp of the body. If your eyes are healthy, your whole body will be full of light. But if your eyes are unhealthy, your whole body will be full of darkness. If then the light within you is darkness, how great is that darkness!"

MATTHEW 6:22-23 (NIV)

Turn on the light so you can see.

I have always wondered at the verses in Matthew 6 that direct us to have good eyes full of light. It seems obvious to me that we all want to walk in the light, otherwise we stumble and fall. We knock against furniture, walk into doors, or fall on our faces. Darkness can be scary. I want to turn the lights on so I can see.

I remember my Dad playing hide and seek with me as a child in our old farmhouse in Niagara-on-the-Lake, Ontario. I loved the suspense of finding him, but I didn't like the dark spaces underneath the stairwell where I had to search to find him. Even remembering makes my palms sweat! The darkness and the unknown caused an adrenaline surge that was exciting and scary all at the same time. Turning on the lights brought out the truth of where we were hiding, and that ended the fear. How amazing it would have been if the interior light of God could have shone out my eyeballs like a flashlight. Then, walking into those dark places wouldn't have been so scary.

The eye is the lamp of the body. If it is healthy and full of light, my whole perception and life will be full of light. If I am focused on what is unhealthy, my whole life will be full of darkness. That's what Jesus said. Taking this a step further, I could say that darkness will increase my fear, anxiety, and worry responses, similar to what I experienced playing hide and seek, but without the excitement and anticipation of seeking and finding.

So what am I filling my eyes with? Light or darkness?

In ancient times, they would have asked this question differently. In that time, people understood that "sight was a process where light passed out of the body through the eyes."[1] The question would not have been, what is entering my eyes but, what is shining from my heart through my eyes? Is my interior life or heart filled with light or darkness? As an ancient citizen living in Jesus' time, I would have understood that what Jesus was talking about was my interior life. In fact, the entire Sermon on the Mount was not about external behaviour directly but about the heart issues that drive behaviour.

In simplest terms, Jesus cares about what is happening within us. He wants our interior lives filled with Him—His light and His love—so that what pours out will be light. Jethani comments: "To change the way we see the world, Jesus is saying that our inner light—our heart—is what needs transformation."[2]

Now, let's go back to darkness for a minute. The www.gotquestions. org website puts it like this: "If we are in a lighted room, we see everything clearly. We can move around obstacles and locate whatever we're looking for. But walking in darkness results in stumbling, falling, and groping for some secure thing to hang on to."[3]

We are left "groping for some secure thing to hang on to."

I ask myself, what am I groping for when the unknowns around money, debt, and possessions overwhelm me? I wonder if it isn't worry. I hang on to worry because it is a familiar place to store fear. Instead of stretching my hand out to God in vulnerable trust, crying out to Him in all of my uncertainties, I recoil back into the place of comfortable and corroding worry, filling my mind with more thoughts of darkness. My inner trust in God isn't determining my response, my inner fear is.

What a reality this is in my life. It makes me want to shout at myself and cry out and beseech all of you in this moment—wake up to the darkness that you see! Worry is not a faithful friend but an ancient deceiver that brings no life. It adds nothing; it only strips life away.

> AS AN ANCIENT CITIZEN LIVING IN JESUS' TIME, I WOULD HAVE UNDERSTOOD THAT WHAT JESUS WAS TALKING ABOUT WAS MY INTERIOR LIFE. IN FACT, THE ENTIRE SERMON ON THE MOUNT WAS NOT ABOUT EXTERNAL BEHAVIOUR DIRECTLY BUT ABOUT THE HEART ISSUES THAT DRIVE BEHAVIOUR.

As I cry out for truth in this area, and as I write about worry and the freedom God has for us as we trust Him more and more, I realize my eyes need light daily. Hour by hour. Minute by minute. I realize I need to focus on what will drive away the darkness and fill my sight with light, all the while understanding that what needs transformation is my heart. I need to see Christ and Him crucified. I need—I want—to see my resurrected Lord, the Author of life and love. I want to see and remember and draw near to Him. He is my focal point for He is the Light of the World that drives back the darkness. He doesn't leave me. He doesn't leave you. He is the light, and He continually calls us back to Himself as the Light of the World. It is His light within me that makes my eyes healthy and strong. I guess it is like that story of hide and seek with my father so long ago. Without light I stay in fear and darkness, but with light I find the truth, and fear is dispelled.

Jesus said, "I am the light of the world. Whoever follows me will never walk in darkness, but will have the light of life" (John 8:12, NIV). That is the truth I want God to embed within me.

MEDITATE: MATTHEW 6:22-23, PHILIPPIANS 4:8

CULTIVATING COMMUNION

Today I want you to sit in the dark for a while to reacquaint yourself with darkness. You may have to wait until evening so that you can sit in complete darkness. As you sit, consider how well you can see and how this darkness affects your ability to read, to cook, to create, to do laundry. Can you complete these tasks? Now consider how worry and fear—as the friends of darkness—hamper your ability to carry out daily tasks and activities. Consider how worry and fear cloud and hinder your sight. Do worry and fear help you see clearly?

Then, after 10 minutes, turn on the lights. How well can you see? Can you read, cook, create, do laundry? Now consider the Light of Christ and how His truth, hope, and words bring light into your life—flow out of your life. Does His light "add" anything to your ability to live your life? Take some time. Journal what you are learning at this moment so that the next time you find yourself troubled or worried about money, you can more easily remember to turn to Him and be filled with His Light and Truth.

Note: Earlier on, I mentioned the acronym **FACE** that we often use in financial coaching: Financial **A**wareness **C**reates **E**mpowerment. My husband and financial coach, David, says that when we aren't facing our finances, we are completely in the dark. He says:

> We walk in financial darkness because we are often afraid to look. Over a long period of time this is disastrous. Bills pile up and we get deeper into trouble. In my brain, it is the fear of looking that brings disaster. Turning the light on in your finances is actually going to bring freedom. If you can **FACE** it, you may discover that your situation isn't as bad as you thought. And if it is, then you can seek the help you need to make a plan. So often, we have seen people gain freedom simply by having the courage to turn the lights on in their finances.

Be Anxious For Nothing

"Be anxious for nothing, but in everything by prayer and supplication, with thanksgiving, let your requests be made known to God; and the peace of God, which surpasses all understanding, will guard your hearts and minds through Christ Jesus."

PHILIPPIANS 4:6-7 (NKJV)

"Be anxious for nothing." This phrase gives me pause today. As we live and work in a global pandemic, I have started to wonder whether a worry-free life is really possible. I know! I know! How can I even mention this in the middle of our study about being unleashed and freed from worry into deeper trust with God? It's bad timing to ask.

But do you ever wonder?

Sometimes I feel pressure to live a life that is burden-free, worry-free. "If I really trust Jesus I will be like a mountain goat leaping across the mountains," I say to myself, without considering that the mountain goat walks in very steep, high places, lined with crevices, falling rocks, and narrow pathways.

In the midst of Covid-19, as vaccinations are rolling out across Canada, the future remains uncertain on many levels. We are in our third wave in Ontario and remain locked down. People have lost jobs and income, and health is a constant concern. People are feeling angry, burdened, sorrowful, even depressed. Worry and anxiety fill the atmosphere. This is a challenging season for many, even as Christ-followers. Many of us are asking how we can bear the light and hope of Christ in such a time as this. How do we share the good news of Jesus when so many eyes are filled with darkness?

I don't know if this expectation to be "light as a feather" comes from within me or from some unwritten expectation I get from Scripture—that I hear in Philippians 4 and in Matthew 11.

Philippians 4:6-7 says, "Do not be anxious about anything, but in every situation, by prayer and petition, with thanksgiving, present your requests to God. And the peace of God, which transcends all understanding, will guard your hearts and your minds in Christ Jesus" (NIV).

Matthew 11:28-30 says, "Come to me, all you who are weary and burdened, and I will give you rest. Take my yoke upon you and learn from me, for I am gentle and humble in heart, and you will find rest for your souls. For my yoke is easy and my burden is light" (NIV).

> SOMETIMES I FEEL PRESSURE TO LIVE A LIFE THAT IS BURDEN-FREE, WORRY-FREE. "IF I REALLY TRUST JESUS I WILL BE LIKE A MOUNTAIN GOAT LEAPING ACROSS THE MOUNTAINS," I SAY TO MYSELF, WITHOUT CONSIDERING THAT THE MOUNTAIN GOAT WALKS IN VERY STEEP, HIGH PLACES, LINED WITH CREVICES, FALLING ROCKS, AND NARROW PATHWAYS.

As we have learned, worry adds nothing to our lives. Jesus does tell us clearly not to worry about our lives, about what we will eat, drink, or wear. We have been learning some practical ways to shed that worry by looking at the birds of the air, remembering our Creator, meditating on who He is, and giving thanks.

So as I wonder whether a worry-free life is possible, I look to these Scriptures including, again, Matthew 6. I hear God remind me that He is offering me an exchange for my worries: peace for anxiety; rest for weariness. It assures and blesses me to know that God, in His wisdom, understands what anxiety and worry can do to me. Again, He doesn't leave us helpless. He invites us to come near Him in prayer and supplication, all the while giving thanks. He invites us to prayer and rest. He invites us to come to Him because His peace and His rest are promised.

In Philippians 4:13, the Apostle Paul tells us that he can do all things through Christ who gives him strength. Today, this reminds me that the "all things through Christ" may apply to me too. Perhaps a worry-free life is possible even in the midst of a pandemic because God, who has promised, is faithful to Himself, His promises, and to us. If He invites me to come for rest and to lay down my anxieties, He is faithful to meet me in this place of weariness and anxiety. He doesn't just ask me to come, He shows me how to make the exchange.

MEDITATE: MATTHEW 11:28-30, PHILIPPIANS 4:4-13

CULTIVATING COMMUNION

Reflect on whether or not you are ready to release your worries about your finances to God. Consider what God instructs us to do with our anxiety and weariness based on the verses above. Take a piece of blank paper and write down your worries and what is making you tired. Picture Jesus sitting with you. He is hearing you and He is reaching out with His hands to take your worries and weariness. Crumple the piece of paper in your hand and lay it aside, as if you are putting it in His hands. What do you imagine He would say to you about what you are sharing with Him? If you want, write the words down. This may not erase or lift your worries and burdens right away, but maybe it is a practice you can continue as you learn and grow.

Here's another idea I have practised with my youngest daughter, Serena, at the end of the day. Imagine you are putting all of your cares in a backpack. You name each worry, care, and fear, and put it in your imaginary backpack. Then you offer that backpack to Jesus. Picture Him taking it from you. This has been a visual and practical exercise that has helped Serena and me release ourselves to God's care even in our sleep. You may be tempted to retrieve that backpack from Christ as you find yourself meditating and thinking about those financial concerns you don't yet have answers to. Give yourself some grace. Re-focus on Christ, then hand it all back to Him—as often as you need to. Remember, learning deeper trust in God is a journey.

Trust in the Lord

"Trust in the Lord forever, for the Lord, the Lord Himself, is the Rock Eternal."

Isaiah 26:4 (NIV)

Trust.

This is a powerful, mysterious five letter word.

We all trust in something. According to the Psalmist, some trust in horses, some in chariots, but some trust in the name of the Lord (see Psalm 20:7).

Love.

This is a powerful, mysterious four letter word.

We all love something. According to the Apostle Paul, if we don't have love, all the other knowledge, gifts, and training amount to nothing (see 1 Corinthians 13).

Worship.

This is a powerful, mysterious seven letter word.

We all worship something. According to Jesus, God is Spirit and His worshipers must worship in Spirit and in truth (see John 4:24).

Trust. Love. Worship. In cultivating trust in our lives, we come to love the one we trust and, then, worship that one. If we trust in money, our happiness and fulfillment will depend on it. We will focus on money as the source of our provision. Our trust in it will lead us to pursue it and pour our attention and time into getting more of it. Money will occupy our thinking and become the focus of what we worship as long as it provides what we want and expect. However, if money lets us down by drying up due to job loss or life circumstances, worry and anxiety are the outcomes. Money will prove untrustworthy in such cases, and we will be left rudderless on the tide.

My husband and financial coach, David, says there are deeper issues at play. It's more than trusting money. At the root of it, it's about how we put trust in ourselves. He says:

> I think we need to understand that we put our trust in a person: either Jesus or ourselves. If you think about putting trust in money, I am not sure that is accurate. We put our trust in ourselves—our own ability to make money. It's putting trust in ME instead of God. The garden story speaks to this origin. Adam and Eve heard the voice of doubt—"Did God really say?" In that doubt, they took their eyes off God and wondered if He was trustworthy. It is the same for us today. In our doubt, we take our eyes off God and trust our own ability to steer the ship. Same question. Same doubt. Same result.

No matter what or whom we trust, or what we tell ourselves about what or whom we trust, we are always cultivating trust in something. We may not look to money as the source of our happiness, but perhaps we rely on something or someone else.

I don't think I understood my own trust in money and possessions until David left the family business and started financial coaching. It wasn't until worry and fear reared their ugly heads that I began to understand that my trust lay in the wrong thing. I have loved the Lord almost my whole life but, when we were left without a sustainable income for over a year, three main truths came to light for me.

1. I was putting trust in my bank account, in the family business to provide an income, and in David to meet my needs.
2. Worry was the fruit of that trust.
3. I wasn't trusting God for provision, but I knew I wanted to.

I know we need to work and provide for our lives, our shelter, and our families. Ecclesiastes is filled with verses that encourage us to enjoy the fruit of our labour. But that wisdom book also reminds us not to put trust in our hard work or in the good things we enjoy, because life is short. God wants us to work and provide for our families, but He wants us to trust Him more than we trust ourselves. When David and I started our journey with More Than Enough, we knew God was revealing our need for Him as our only Source of provision. David and I needed deep-water trust in God Himself, not in anything else or anyone else, to walk the journey we were about to embark on.

Let me give you some context.

Up until the past few years, as I have started working in our business, we have been a single-income, homeschooling family. The only financial advice we were given when we were married was to "live" on one salary and "play" on the other. In those early years, I finished my political science and journalism bachelor's degree and worked for a few years. We went on trips, lived simply, invested some, and "played" on my part-time salary as a reporter at a community newspaper. Then, when we had kids six years into our marriage, we decided I would stay home. We didn't need to shift too much in our finances because we were already living off of just one salary. In those days, we didn't have financial dates or do our money meetings together. Dave worked 12 hours a day and left the managing of the household and our personal finances to me. We prayed often for needs we had and looked to the Lord for practical things like vehicles, bunk beds, and clothing for the kids. When David left the family business, we felt like God was calling us to walk on water and trust Him in ways we hadn't before. We submitted our ideas, strengths, bank accounts, and our talents and abilities to Him. David so often came home on Friday nights wondering what a mechanic was doing as a financial coach, especially with the personal financial stresses that came with this life. Here we were trying to trust God, starting up a financial coaching company, and helping others navigate their finances when we ourselves were making just enough money to cover our own expenses. We had a lot of questions, but we kept turning to God as our Source and Provider. There was a lot of waiting and a lot of lament, but we kept putting one foot in front of the other, in obedience, as we trusted His voice.

Isaiah 31 says, "Woe to those who go down to Egypt for help, who rely on horses, who trust in the multitude of their chariots, and in the great strength of their horsemen, but do not look to the Holy One of Israel, or seek help from the Lord."

David and I, along with our kids, were learning to seek help from the Lord and not look to, or go back to, what we trusted before—the place we called Egypt. We were learning that God's economy is His own: mysterious, powerful, and always full of provision. We learned some valuable lessons. When we stopped trusting in the ways of Egypt and our past provision, we found what we needed in the most unlikely places, usually funneled through the hands of others. David did what he could by driving a limousine and doing odd jobs here and there, but our focus was on this place of More Than Enough that He had given us. We began to put our hand in God's and look to Him for help, both for physical and spiritual nourishment.

There is a story Jesus tells in the Gospels. A wise man goes to build a house on rock. He digs deep, pours a foundation, then builds his home. His house is built on sturdy rock so that, when the storms come and rage, the house stands. The foolish man, however, spends his time, resources, and money building a house on sand. When the storms come, his house falls (see Luke 6:46-49).

David and I have been learning hour by hour, day by day, year by year, that God is our Provider. We have been learning to dig deep and build our house on the foundation stone, the cornerstone of Jesus Christ and His promises. We aren't doing this with perfection, but we do it with willingness, tenacity, and intention. The more we trust, the more we have grown to love Him with all of who we are. This has also led to deeper worship. He is so faithful. He is so tender in His care. He is so loving. I may not always understand His ways, but I am knowing and loving Him more and expressing more of my love to Him.

That is the trust, the love, and the worship growing in my life and, I hope, in you too.

MEDITATE: PSALM 127:1, LUKE 6:46-49, MATTHEW 6:25-30

CULTIVATING COMMUNION

I am thinking of the words my brother, Dave, shared when we talked about cultivating farmland and trust in the Lord. He said that trusting God is not a magic formula. We can go to the Scriptures and find His promises of provision, love, and care, but it is up to us to find them and weave them into our thinking and being. This faith in His promises is something we pray for, but it is also something we build into our lives as we read His Word.

What—or who—are you trusting in this season? Do you carry any worries that are indicating a lack of trust in God's love, care, and provision? Look at the promises of the Scriptures above. Write down and pray about one word that jumps out to you. What is the promise from the Lord? What is He promising you? Reflect on that word and give Him thanks.

SIDE BAR:
Remember Your Creator

My friend Pam (whom you have already met earlier in this book) recently posted a message encouraging us not to worry. Here is what she wrote, as if the Lord Himself was speaking to us:

Why are you worrying? Worrying doesn't add anything to your life. Remember to "cast onto Me," those questions, concerns, and fears that your flesh wants to focus on. Yes, it can feel "foolish" not to worry because you think it's making you more aware, but in reality, the worry you give in to, simply clouds or covers the peace that I have for you. Remember, My peace isn't something that always makes sense to the world or your flesh—it just IS! It's a tribute and a testament to the truth that I am always with you—that I am aware, that I am big enough, and that I am more than enough to handle what the world throws at you. Rest. Peace. Worry less—pray more. Fret less—praise more. (Pam Dyck, Facebook post, June 9, 2021)

Her post made me think of the words from Ecclesiastes 12:1: "Remember also your Creator in the days of your youth, before the evil days come and the years draw near of which you say, 'I have no pleasure in them.'"

Remember your Creator. In his book, *Living Life Backward,* David Gibson tells us that the "fallenness of the created order has not removed all its goodness and beauty. If we live as if it has, then we have forgotten the Creator."[1] I want to suggest that in our focus on all that is wrong with the world, including our finances, our focus has slipped from worshipping and giving thanks to God as Creator, to the place where we have become self-absorbed and self-focused as if we are in charge of our own lives. When we forget that we have a Creator who loves us, we enter into cycles of worry, fretting, and anxiety, and we focus on our own abilities to problem solve instead of welcoming and inviting God to play His role in our stories. "If grumpiness grows with the sin of ingratitude, anxiety flourishes with the sin of idolatry. It is fertilized by the belief that I am in charge of my life and must do all I can to control my circumstances."[2]

Jesus Himself reminds us in Matthew 6 to look at creation. Remember the birds. Remember the lilies of the field. Remember your Creator. I think He is urging us to remember we are the created ones, not would-be creators. He reminds us throughout the Sermon on the Mount that we have a Father who cares for us. Releasing ourselves again and again to this truth may help us in our journey of trust, remembering who He is and who we are. There is so much in our lives we cannot change, so surrendering to our Creator King seems the prudent option and the most direct path to peace.

Worship What You Love

"Trust in the Lord with all your heart, and lean not on your own understanding. In all your ways submit to Him and He will make your paths straight."

PROVERBS 3:5-6 (NIV)

"You will keep in perfect peace those whose minds are steadfast because they trust in You. Trust in the Lord forever, for the Lord, the Lord Himself, is the Rock Eternal."

ISAIAH 26:3-4 (NIV)

"Let the morning bring me word of your unfailing love, for I have put my trust in You. Show me the way I should go, for to You I entrust my life."

PSALM 143:8 (NIV)

Trust. Love. Worship. Three mysterious and powerful words. And with those words come the questions that we have already been looking at.
- Whom or what do I trust?
- Whom or what do I love?
- Whom or what do I worship?

I have been reading an interesting book called *You Are What You Love: The Spiritual Power of Habit,* by James K.A. Smith. He says that to worship is human but what we truly love and worship isn't necessarily what we think we love and worship. It's **not** an issue of whether we worship, it's *what we* worship.[1]

Writer David Foster Wallace agrees:

In the day-to-day trenches of adult life, there is no such thing as atheism. There is no such thing as not worshipping. Everybody worships. The only choice we get is what to worship... If you worship money and things—if they are where you tap real meaning in life—then you will never have enough. Never feel you have enough. It's the truth. Worship your own body and beauty and sexual allure and you will always feel ugly, and when time and age start showing, you will die a million deaths before they finally plant you. On one level, we all know this stuff already—it's been codified as myths, proverbs, cliches, bromides, epigrams, parables: the skeleton of every great story. The trick is keeping the truth up front in daily consciousness.[2]

For a Christ-follower, trusting, loving, and worshipping anything other than our Lord and Saviour is idolatry. Author, speaker, and coach Dr. Steve Brown says that idolatry takes different forms in our culture, but acts like a spiritual bungee cord in our lives, always drawing us back into woundedness and sin. "At its root is the misplaced worship of and false trust in something we have created and prized rather than God. When we seek our identity, security and hope in something or someone other than God, we are engaging in idolatry."[3]

So where am I seeking my security, my hope, and my identity? What North Star is my heart using for navigation? Our habits can tell us a great deal. They reveal what is at the heart of our trust and worship. Is my North Star and source of security found in forms of religious duty, escapist entertainment, workaholism, alcoholism, pornography, shopping, eating, drinking, schooling, career advancement, or is my North Star God Himself? According to Smith, our habits are filled with formative practices that tune our hearts to sing the songs of the world around us and not the songs of God. Our loves are habits that operate "under the hood" so to speak. "Some cultural practices will be effectively training your loves, automating a kind of orientation to the world that seeps into your unconscious ways of being. That's why you might not love what you think."[4]

What song, then, are you singing? What habits are helping you navigate this life? Maybe you have never looked at your life in this way before so these may be new and important questions for you to consider. They may even be overwhelming questions for you. Whether you are prepared to consider and answer these questions today, or whether these questions overwhelm you, I want to offer this hope: in training our habits, our loves, and ensuring worry and anxiety do not overtake us, we can lay hold of the hope of Jesus Himself, knowing that He walked this earth just as we are, and He has an endless supply of wisdom and compassion to help us love Him most.

He. Is. Our. Hope.

In Hebrews, God tells us that we can flee for refuge to "lay hold of the hope set before us." It is a hope that is an "anchor of the soul, both sure and steadfast." That anchor is Jesus (see Hebrews 6:18-20, NKJV). Jesus. That beautiful name. Our intimate friend and Lord. In the midst of all the navigating of loves and habits, understanding what we worship and what we don't, we have Jesus. In the midst of the worries that rise in our sometimes faithless hearts, we have Jesus.

Proverbs 3 tells us to trust in the Lord with all of our hearts, and not to lean on our own understanding, but to acknowledge and submit to God in everything, and He will straighten our paths. Isaiah 26 says that God will keep us in perfect peace because we trust in Him. We gain SO MUCH when we even attempt to put God first in everything. His word to us is that He keeps us when we turn to Him in trust. He will keep us in perfect peace. Hebrews again tells us that we can "hold fast this confession of hope without wavering" because God is faithful to keep His promises. We can boldly come to the throne of grace to obtain mercy and grace in time of need (see Hebrews 10:23 & 4:16). Jesus is our hope. As He was tempted "in all points as we are, yet without sin," we know He sympathizes with us as we attempt to trust God, love Him most, and worship Him alone (see Hebrews 4:14).

When we recognize our habits, our faithlessness, our divided hearts, and the worldly masters we try to serve, we can run back to Him. We run back in trust because we know that the faithful arms of God are arms of forgiveness, love, and hope. This journey of trust, love, and worship is exactly that—a journey. You don't need to have it all figured out. He has it figured out and He will show you the way.

MEDITATE: PSALM 143:8, PROVERBS 3:5-6, ISAIAH 26:3

CULTIVATING COMMUNION

Using the words of writer David Foster Wallace, where do you "tap" real meaning in life?[5] Is it from your walk with God, or do you sense that some of your habits in life are telling a different story about what you trust, love, and worship? Take some time now to consider whether you are singing the songs of the world or God's songs. Of course this is a metaphor, but it is an extremely helpful metaphor and encourages us to use our voices in praise to God. Singing songs of worship and praise are essential ways of forming habits and practices within us that orientate us to the North Star of Jesus Christ. While repentance is essential in these considerations (you can read about that at the end of this book), vocal worship is also wonderfully important. Tell God where you are at but also thank Him, praise Him, and worship Him with songs of praise and thanksgiving like, "How Great Thou Art," "Holy, Holy, Holy, Lord God Almighty," "My Lighthouse," by Rend Collective, or "Good Good Father," by Chris Tomlin. Do it alone, do it with family, or do it within the community of believers.

As we open ourselves up to worship Him, we are taking our eyes off ourselves and opening ourselves up to the revelation, divine presence, and visitation of God. Smith says that worship is a site of God's action not just God's presence. He writes:

> God is the first and primary actor in worship. But the point isn't passivity, turning us into a mere audience, spectators of what Someone Else is doing...Instead, this emphasis on God's action in worship includes a picture of graced interaction between God and his people, a liturgical form of call and response, grace and gratitude."[6]

When we worship God there is an interaction between God and us, where He is inviting us to participate. I believe it is in this place where we re-orientate ourselves to Him as the Source of our lives. It is a place where worship of Him becomes a tool of trust cultivation.

A Meandering Path: From Worry to Prayer

"There is so much fear in us. Fear of people, fear of God and much raw, undefined, free-floating anxiety. I wonder if fear is not our main obstacle to prayer. When we enter into the presence of God and start to sense that huge reservoir of fear in us, we want to run away into the many distractions which our busy world offers us so abundantly. But we should not be afraid of our fears. We can confront them, give words to them and lead them into the presence of Him who says: 'Do not be afraid, it is I.' Our inclination is to show our Lord only what we feel comfortable with. But the more we dare to reveal our whole trembling self to Him, the more we will be able to sense that His love, which is perfect love, casts out all our fears."

HENRI J.M. NOUWEN, WRITER AND THEOLOGIAN, FROM *A CRY FOR MERCY*

Our journey to More Than Enough was a meandering path. It started with moving from the village of Winchester to our 'dream' home on a country road with 25 acres of land, only a few miles away. Selling our home and buying our log home was an unexpected journey of trust and learning that grew deeper roots of faith for both me and David. The move took place August 5th, 2006, and led to great physical exhaustion for both of us. I remember the week following—simply lying on the couch because I couldn't move. Little did we know or understand that this was just the beginning of a new, hard, and wonderfully surprising journey into the heart of God.

Fast forward to September 2007. Those were David's last days working in the family's automotive business where he worked as manager. His exit happened on that September long weekend and, as we left, we didn't know where we were going. We had savings but we had no idea how we would support our family. We simply followed the soft voice of God that continually nudged us: "It's time to go. Follow me."

So, we followed.

And a few months later, David started working with Lynn Fraser to create the More Than Enough Financial Coaching program. At the beginning, there were financial needs in our lives that many start-up entrepreneurs would understand. It was now February 2008, and we needed to make an intentional plan about our personal financial situation. We had four children and a mortgage, so we looked at our savings accounts and determined we would run out of money by August. Sitting here writing this, I don't remember the feelings of worry, but I know they were there. This journey was fraught with obstacles and questions: "Is this really the place You want us to be Lord?" Many Friday evenings, David would come home discouraged. He was working outside his wheelhouse and comfort zone. So was I. How did this automotive technician find himself as a financial coach?

For our own finances and direction, we decided to fast and pray. We didn't realize we were turning our worries to prayer but that's exactly what we were doing. We also asked our prayer team* to pray with us. And what was our request? "Should David get a part-time job so we could pay the bills and extend the savings we were using to live?" We homeschooled our children and, honestly, it hadn't occurred to us that I should look for work—that's how committed we were to being with our kids. So we spent the weekend praying and, by the end of our time with God, we sensed His still small voice reassuring us and encouraging David to keep coaching, to pursue no other work, and to stay focused at More Than Enough. The overall message from the Lord we sensed was, *"Trust Me."*

So, Monday morning we got out of bed and continued on. Obedience had become David's watch word as he continued to walk out this new call of helping people find hope and freedom with God in finances. We were putting everything before the Lord. Even our home. We knew that if we needed to sell it as part of this obedience, we would. However, selling our home was not the answer. God had another plan. As I stood in the laundry room, folding and separating clothes that morning, a friend called with an unexpected question: "How are you guys doing financially?" It's not a question you get asked every day and, up to this point, we had not shared any of our financial needs with others. I didn't really know what to say. We had food for the week, a warm house, and beds to sleep in. We were grateful in spite of all the uncertainty.

"Well, the reason I am calling is because my husband and I were praying for you this weekend," she said. "When we each had our quiet time with God we both felt directed to pay your mortgage for the rest of the year. We want you to understand that God spoke to us separately about this. When we were chatting about you this morning, we realized we had heard the same message. So, how much is your mortgage so I can send you some cheques?"

I didn't know what to say. I started crying. This was such an immediate answer. While we were praying that weekend, God was orchestrating something we hadn't imagined. Having the mortgage paid for the year released the financial strain. David started drawing in more income, and we continued to make it all work. God was making a way.

There have been hundreds of other ways, and people, He has used to support and provide for us over these years. God hasn't always answered us as immediately as this, and He doesn't always send a cheque in the mail. However, God is nothing if not creative, and we have been amazed time and again by His care. There have been situations that have pushed our trust to deeper levels because we didn't see the answers we desired, nor in the timeframe we wanted them, but He has answered and continues to do so. Coming to Him in prayer, with my worries, anxieties, and fears has been essential for my relationship with Him, and for our relationship with Him as a couple, as business owners, and as a family. We have grown in love and trust. We have seen

Him answer because, as it says in 2 Timothy 2:13, "If we are faithless, He remains faithful. He cannot deny Himself" (NKJV). It is because of His love and faithfulness that we can cast all our cares upon Him for He cares for us (see 1 Peter 5:7). That is a promise I can hang on to.

MEDITATE: MATTHEW 11:28-30, PHILIPPIANS 4:4-7, EPHESIANS 3:14-21

CULTIVATING COMMUNION

1 Peter 5:7 says that we can cast all our cares upon God because He cares for us. Today, tell him what you are worried about. Pour out your "cry of the heart" prayers, as John Eldredge calls them.** Wait and see how He will answer.

Understand that you are in training to trust Him for your daily bread. You are on a journey of trust, learning even in the worry to keep looking up to Him. Keep drawing yourself to His side. Then when you see the answer(s), tell someone or write them down. Give God the glory He deserves. As our colleague and More Than Enough entrepreneurial coach, Bron Vasic, often asks, "what is the glory that God wants you to experience through this experience?" Remember He wants you to experience His glory as you turn from the things of this world and look completely to Him.

*What is a prayer team? Over the years, we have asked and gathered people to pray for More Than Enough. The team is made up of people who love us and feel called to support us in this way. I regularly send a prayer letter out to a larger group of friends who pray, and I meet once a week with a smaller group of women who have been praying with me for almost 20 years. If you own a business, lead a family, have a ministry, or are a child of God, having people pray for you regularly is so wonderfully

> THERE HAVE BEEN SITUATIONS THAT HAVE PUSHED OUR TRUST TO DEEPER LEVELS BECAUSE WE DIDN'T SEE THE ANSWERS WE DESIRED, IN THE TIMEFRAME WE WANTED THEM, BUT HE HAS ANSWERED AND CONTINUES TO DO SO.

helpful and inspiring. I would encourage you to find at least two people who will commit to praying for you and, sometimes, with you. One of our dearest intercessors prays with David three mornings a week at 8 a.m. It doesn't have to be a long prayer time, but doing it regularly brings blessing, accountability, and answers to so many of the challenges we face daily.

**John Eldredge, director at Ransomed Heart Ministries, says some prayers just happen. "They are 'the Cry of the Heart.' No training is needed when it comes to this kind of prayer. I've uttered it thousands of times; I'm confident you have too. Like when the phone rings and the bad news starts to spill and all you can do is say, Father ... Father ... Father, your heart crying out to God. It's a beautiful expression of prayer, rising from the deep places in us, often unbidden, always welcome to His loving ears."[1]

Best Laid Plans

Dread traveled slowly down the back of my neck and along my spine to the tips of my extremities. My knees threatened to buckle beneath me as waves of nausea washed over me. The woman I was speaking with had just uttered words confirming God's new plan for my life, and the life of my family.

For the better part of a year, my son had been asking to be homeschooled. I was a stay-at-home mom at the time, but the plan for our immediate future did not include homeschooling. The plan was that I would enter the workforce once my youngest started school full-time, which happened to be at the end of the summer.

As I was sitting with my son one evening, he suddenly turned to me, looked me in the eye, and demanded to know why I would not homeschool him. I was taken aback, tongue-tied by the ferocity behind the question. What could I say? My mind raced trying to figure out an explanation that would make sense to him. I didn't want to explain our financial situation so, in desperation, I grabbed at my go-to answer for all big decisions—we would pray together and ask God whether He wanted me to homeschool him. In the back of my mind, I was certain that God would clearly direct me to go back to work.

Wrong! God answered our prayer but not in the way I wanted or expected. I was to homeschool my son and not work. As my husband and I got our minds around this new turn of events, I realized I'd better take a good look at our budget as there would be no second income come September, as we'd planned. We had tightened our belt for many years, and I knew there were few areas that could be massaged, pruned, or cut.

I gave the calculator a workout as I tried to get the expense side of the budget to match the revenue side, but no matter how hard I tried, I was short by $100 per month. It was an impossible task. I turned to God and asked for His help to balance the budget.

Several days later, as I was delivering materials to one of the Sunday School teachers, she mentioned that she was looking for

someone to clean her home. As we talked, I realized that this was something I could do—and still homeschool my son. I immediately offered my services and was hired for the position. Can you guess what it paid? $100 per month—exactly what we needed.

There is a verse in the Bible that tells us to seek God first and not to worry about the rest. Knowing that verse and living that verse are two very different things. Our homeschooling season taught me and my husband that when we put God's plan for our lives first, we can trust Him to provide for our every need—not just our financial ones.

NANCY STEELE
WINCHESTER, ONTARIO, 2021

Navigating the Obstacles

"Obstacles are sometimes the best opportunities."
YAIRUS PUBLISHING HOUSE

I saw this photo recently of a beautiful, budding, deciduous tree growing up through the front steps of a whitewashed country home. As I imagined sitting beneath that tree, I could almost taste the lemonade and hear the crickets sing. In my mind, it was a perfect place for rest. Yet, it was also odd. The tree was growing up through the front porch, and it triggered an inner need to get David's chainsaw and cut it down! What was a tree doing growing up through that porch?

"Obstacles are sometimes the best opportunities." That's what Yairus Publishing House posted underneath that photo on a social media post in May 2021. "At Yairus Publishing we see these 'obstacles' as part of the creative process. As your story develops, allow the things that you didn't plan for, or feel like barriers, to become part of your masterpiece."[1]

Of course, they are speaking to authors, but it got me wondering if any of you look at your financial obstacles in this way. You open the front door and find a tree shooting up through your front porch. It wasn't there yesterday, but it's there today. What do you do? Do you welcome the hindrances as potential opportunities in your own life's masterpiece? How do you turn financial obstacles into opportunities? What will these "obstacles" become? How are they an "opportunity" for growth, transition, and transformation in our spiritual, relational, and financial lives?

I love the song by TobyMac called "Help is On the Way (Maybe Midnight)"[2]. It reminds me of God's faithfulness, His response to prayers, and His plan for my life. I have seen God turn what I thought were obstacles into opportunities for growth and deeper relationship with Him. As I have already shared, our journey from a family business to More Than Enough had many of those obstacles and opportunities. In retrospect, they became stepping stones for where we are today. We may have had our share of troubles, but the Lord has been faithful to sustain us, to feed us, and to walk with us. Like the imagery of the song suggests, God was "rolling up His sleeves again" to answer and come to our aid.[3] Help was on the way, and it still is!

A few weeks ago, this truth came home to me again. I heard a story about the Miracle of Dunkirk that took place in the early days of World War II. Over 300,000 Allied soldiers were evacuated from the beaches of Dunkirk, France between May 26th and June 4th, 1940. "At the time, Prime Minister Winston Churchill called it *'a miracle of deliverance.'*"[4] The British Expeditionary Force, along with French, Canadian, and Belgian troops, had been fighting the Germans against overwhelming odds. They retreated to the beaches and harbours at Dunkirk but soon realized they were trapped. They had become easy targets. It was determined that, with the positioning of the German troops, the Allied Forces could maybe save 30,000 soldiers, but any more was beyond their hope. It was in this crisis that King George VI called a National Day of Prayer, asking the people of Britain to gather and pray for strength and guidance for the days ahead.[5] People responded by gathering in churches and coming to their knees:

> That very day, the evacuation began. Hundreds of boats set out across the English Channel in a rescue attempt, vulnerable to attack—but unseasonal storms meant the Nazi air force was grounded and unable to fly. Additionally, Hitler had ordered his ground forces to halt, and they didn't move for three days. This combination of events meant that the evacuations were able to take place largely uninterrupted for three days, leading to over 338,000 men being rescued—ten times the expected number![6]

This story inspires me to pray. When the obstacles rise, this story reminds me to fall on my knees in humility and remember who God is. He is my ever-present help. He sees what I cannot see. He hears what I cannot hear. I come to Him with dependent expectancy, knowing He will answer my prayers. Trusting God in my spiritual, relational, or financial life doesn't mean I won't feel desperation but, like a North Star, Jesus will keep guiding me back to trust and hope in Him as I wait and pray in those desperate places.

Even as I meditate on these things, I hear the words of Scripture in my head from 1 Corinthians 2:9-10: "Eye has not seen, nor ear heard, nor have entered into the heart of man the things which God has prepared for those who love Him. But God has revealed them to us through His Spirit. For the Spirit searches all things, yes, the deep things of God" (NKJV).

No eye has seen nor ear heard...But God has revealed them to us through His Spirit.

But God.

But God turns obstacles into opportunities, and reveals His glory and wonder through the opportunities He provides. This isn't just about us getting prayers answered but about the revelation of His glory and His Kingdom throughout all of creation. In Isaiah 61, Scripture tells us that He has given us "beauty for ashes, the oil of joy for mourning, the garment of praise for a spirit of heaviness, that they be called trees of righteousness, the planting of the Lord" for the display of His glory and splendour (see Isaiah 61:3, NKJV). He takes brokenness and turns it into beauty for His glory. He takes those front porch trees and turns them into something good and fruit bearing in our lives. In fact, we can take the illustration one step further. As the Scripture states, we are those trees. Whether planted through a front porch or not, He sees us, not as obstacles in His family or Kingdom, but as His beloved children. We are the people whom He pours His love and life-giving potential through. We are those trees, transformed from glory to glory to display

His splendour. How awesome is that!

MEDITATE: I CORINTHIANS 2:1-12, JEREMIAH 33:1-4

CULTIVATING COMMUNION

How do you deal with the obstacles in your life? Do you have trouble seeing them as opportunities? Is there some kind of tree growing up through the front porch of your life, that you don't know what to do about it? Take some time to listen to TobyMac's song on YouTube, read the lyrics below, research more about the Miracle of Dunkirk, or reflect on how God has turned obstacles into opportunities in your own life. It is so easy for me to forget how God has answered prayers and does answer prayers but, if I find myself worried and anxious, I can use those emotions as diagnostics and red flag warnings to turn back to Him and remember who He is, what He does, and how He loves me. You and I aren't obstacles in His Kingdom, but trees that He has planted for His own glorious display!

"Help is On the Way (Maybe Midnight)" lyrics

I heard your heart I see your pain
Out in the dark Out in the rain
Feel so alone Feel so afraid
I heard you pray in Jesus' name

It may be midnight or mid-day
Never early, never late
He gon' stand by what He claim
I've lived enough life to say

Help is on the way (Roundin' the corner)
Help is on the way (Comin' for ya)
Help is on the way (Yeah, yeah)
I've lived enough life to say
Help is on the way

Sometimes it's days, Sometimes it's years
Some face a lifetime, Of falling tears
But He's in the darkness, He's in the cold
Just like the morning, He always shows

Well I've seen my share of troubles
But the Lord ain't failed me yet
So I'm holding onto the promise y'all
That He's rolling up His sleeves again
Rolling up, rolling up, rolling up His sleeves again

He Will See To It

"And Abraham called the name of the place, 'The-Lord-Will-
Provide; as it is said to this day, 'In the Mount of the Lord it shall
be provided.'"

GENESIS 22:14 (NKJV)

God wants to answer you. He wants to hear from you and answer your prayers. He wants to see to the concerns and cares of your life. He is inviting you to trust Him.

Whether or not you are transparent and vulnerable with others, be honest with God. Tell Him what you think, who you are, and what you want. You may wonder why you need to share your anger or fears, joys or victories with Him if He already knows. He knows anyway, so just tell Him. There is no secret He doesn't know, no shortcoming He doesn't want to strengthen, no sin He won't forgive. He wants to hear from you, and more than that—He wants to answer you.

In Revelation 3, Jesus tells us He is knocking at the door of our hearts and lives. It is up to us to open ourselves up to Him. He continually invites us into relationship and friendship because we are made for that relationship with Him, and He wants to respond.

"Behold, I stand at the door and knock. If anyone hears My voice and opens the door, I will come in to him and dine with him, and he with Me." (Revelation 3:20, NKJV).

There are all kinds of reasons why we don't open that door. We hold on to worry and anxiety because maybe we believe He doesn't really care. We feel that worry is all we are left with, so why give it to

Him when He hasn't seemed to answer us in the past? Or maybe He has answered, but we don't like the answers. Building trust in Him is hard when we think He is not answering or when we don't like His answers. Or maybe we have stopped speaking with Him because we are filled with shame and embarrassment over decisions we have made. We don't want to be "found out" so we resist His invitation. On other occasions, we hold back because His responses or "asks" are too hard.

Take Abraham for instance. In Genesis 22, God asks Abraham to take his son Isaac, the promised seed of a great nation, to the land of Moriah and offer him there as a burnt offering on one of the mountains. Basically, God is asking him to kill his son. Abraham arises, prepares for the journey, and takes Isaac with him. If you know this Old Testament story, you know that Abraham does not kill his son on the altar. His hand is restrained by the Angel of the Lord and Abraham finds a ram to sacrifice instead. God provides the ram that becomes the burnt offering of worship. It seems God never intended Isaac's death, and Abraham had passed the test.

As was often the case throughout these personal encounters with God in the Old Testament, Abraham gives a name to this place of sacrifice and provision. "And Abraham called the name of the place, 'The-Lord-Will-Provide'; as it is said to this day, 'In the Mount of the Lord it shall be provided.'" (Genesis 22:14, NKJV). It is in that place that Abraham received the further promise of blessing that through his seed "all the nations of the earth shall be blessed" (see Genesis 22:18).

This is the first time in Scripture we see and hear the name Jehovah Jireh as a name for the Lord. In the New King James Version His name is written *"YHWH Yireh."* As a child, I knew the meaning of this name because of a chorus we sang called "Jehovah Jireh, My Provider." It is the one name of the Lord I will never forget because of that song! In looking further at the text and meaning of the Hebrew word, there seems to be a further nuance to His name. The Hebrew word y^{e}hōvâ yir'ê means *"Jehovah the Lord will see (to it)"*.[1]

I love that name of the Lord. He is Jehovah, the Lord, who will see to it. He provides, and He will see to it. In your life and mine, He will see to it. We can speak to Him. We can hear from Him, and He will see to it. He wants to be in relationship with me. He wants to hear my heart. He wants to answer me. He wants to see to it—in my life. He wants to see me responding in trust even when I don't understand. He wants to hear from me with all my questions and cares. He wants me to cast all my anxieties upon Him because HE WILL SEE TO IT. That is His name as provider—Jehovah Jireh, the God who will see to it.

"Let me see to it."

My own father spoke those words to me when needs arose throughout my life that were beyond my ability to resolve. When I hear those words today, I know that my heavenly Father is speaking His love and care into my life. "I will take care of this situation for you. Don't worry. I will take care of you. I will see to it that the problem is resolved, the issue taken care of, and the way is made. I will see to it, so leave it with Me."

Don't walk this financial road alone. Ask God for help, tell Him your story, seek Him, and knock on His door. He is your Jehovah Jireh. He wants to answer you, but not only that, He wants to provide and see to what troubles and concerns you. This doesn't mean that we don't have to wait for the answer. It doesn't mean that we will have it easy. It doesn't mean that we will always like what He asks or how He answers but, as we draw near to Him and walk in deeper friendship with Him, we may just start trusting Him more—in spite of the answer—so that when He says, "I will see to it," we know He will.

MEDITATE: MATTHEW 7:7-11, GENESIS 22:1-19

CULTIVATING COMMUNION

First part:

"I will see to it." Our God is the One who sees, and He is the One who sees to it. What is something you would like God to take care

of for you? Maybe there is something just too heavy for you in this season. Why don't you journal it out or just start talking about it? Tell God how you would like Him to answer. One thing I have learned from my daughter Serena is how straightforward her requests are when she talks to God.

"Dear Lord, I want a dog."

"Dear Lord, stop Covid-19 so people stop dying and we can see our friends."

"God, help me get my school done with a good attitude."

What is your straight forward request of God today? Remember, He doesn't give stones for bread or serpents when you ask for fish. Just ask (see Matthew 7:9-11).

Second part:

"I will see to it." Is there something in your financial situation that you haven't taken responsibility for? Is there something YOU need to *see to* so that you fulfill your financial responsibilities? Maybe you haven't filed taxes this year. Maybe you haven't given to the charity you committed to at the beginning of the year. Maybe you have fallen behind in your debt repayment. What area needs you to say, "I will see to it." Take some time now and do the next thing needed to fulfill that task.

Always Rejoice

"Be surprised by joy, be surprised by the little flower that shows its beauty in the midst of a barren desert, and be surprised by the immense healing power that keeps bursting forth like springs of fresh water from the depth of our pain."

HENRI J.M. NOUWEN, WRITER AND THEOLOGIAN

Our daughter Serena Joy is the youngest of our children. She came in God's perfect timing as a "surprise gift" to us. You can often hear these words tumble out of my mouth into her ears: "I am so glad Jesus sent you to us." She laughs with me as these words of love and affirmation tickle her ears and her heart. She came as a gift of joy to us in just the right season, but my initial reaction was mixed. I remember the day I called my mom to tell her the news. I was hanging laundry and not quite over the "shock" of being pregnant in my 40s. Serena Joy was coming into our lives in much the same way I had come into my mother's. The youngest of seven children, I came nine years after my siblings. My mom was 43 when I was born. She always told me that she hadn't planned me, but God had. I never felt unwanted because I was wanted. It just wasn't her plan to have another child, and it wasn't mine either. I don't think my mother or I spoke for a good two minutes after I told her the news. All was telephone silence as we grasped together what this had meant for my mom when I came into the world, and what this was going to mean for us.

Unexpected circumstances or life changes can bring about all kinds of reactions. Having a baby in my 40s was a new experience for me, and it came with all kinds of questions and concerns about the future. My plans for the years ahead got derailed. I, then, had a choice: I could choose to complain about it or I could rejoice in it. For those who struggle with fertility as we once did, you may be wondering how I could ever complain about being pregnant. To be honest, I really wasn't tempted to complain, but I was a bit scared and worried. On so many levels, I needed to process this news and the changes that were about to take place. Then there were David's words to me. Initially, he was just as surprised and shocked as I was. He expressed his heart and gut reaction: "Am I going to lose you to morning sickness and breastfeeding for the next two years?" There it was. Twenty years into our marriage he had plans too, that hadn't included raising another child. Thankfully, we worked through these emotions and reactions and, even though I was sick for half of the pregnancy and spent a year nursing this beautiful baby, David didn't ever feel like he had "lost me."

Maybe you can relate to this story where life circumstances take you by surprise. Maybe it is an unexpected job loss; or unexpected house guests who stay longer than anticipated; or unexpected house repairs; or unexpected inheritance money to steward; or unexpected, unexpected, unexpected!

Scripture teaches us in Philippians 4, that along with bringing our worries and anxieties to God in prayer, we are to bring them with thanksgiving. In fact, before we even get to the anxiety instructions, He tells us to rejoice.

> Rejoice in the Lord always. I will say it again: Rejoice! Let your gentleness be evident to all. The Lord is near. Do not be anxious about anything, but in every situation, by prayer and petition, with thanksgiving, present your requests to God. And the peace of God, which transcends all understanding, will guard your hearts and your minds in Christ Jesus (Philippians 4:4-7, NIV).

In the face of uncertainty, rejoice in the Lord. In economic stress, rejoice in the Lord. In more bills than money at the end of each month, rejoice! Rejoice means to take delight or great joy in something. Another way to say this is, "Be glad in the Lord always. Be glad!

Henri J.M. Nouwen says that joy is a choice, and he invites us to choose joy every day and to be surprised by the wonder of joy, even in the midst of hardship:

> Joy does not simply happen to us. We have to choose joy and keep choosing it every day. It is a choice based on the knowledge that we belong to God and have found in God our refuge and our safety and that nothing, not even death, can take God away from us.[1]

Is my gladness based on my circumstances? Is my gladness based on my economic well-being? No. According to Paul's admonition, **our gladness is based in the Lord.** And who is the Lord? He is the Lord of Lords, the King of Kings, my Saviour, my Redeemer, my Resurrection, my Life, my Strength, my Counsellor, my Peace, my Overcomer, my Refuge, my Resting Place, my Deliverer, and so much more.

MEDITATE: PHILIPPIANS 4:4

CULTIVATING COMMUNION

- Write down your specific worry today over an "unexpected" in your life.
- Next to that worry, write out who you know God is and how who He is speaks to that worry.
- Write down what you are hearing Him speak to you in this moment, and rejoice in how He is meeting you in this worry.

Let me give you an example:

- **Worry?** The cost of having another child in my 40s.
- **Who He is?** He is my Counsellor and Wisdom.
- **What does this truth speak?** He will show me the way forward, every step, every day, and I can ask Him for counsel and wisdom when I am afraid. "If any of you lacks wisdom let him ask of God, who gives to all liberally without reproach, and it will be given to him" (James 1:5, NKJV).
- **Rejoice in the Lord.** Thank You for being my Lord. Thank You that You are my Counsellor and Wisdom, not just for all

the world, but for me, today. I am so glad that You are leading me and will lead me in everything as we raise this beautiful baby whom You have given us. I am so glad that You are her Provider, and will give her everything she needs. I am glad in You today. I rejoice that You are my Lord.

The Gift of Gratitude

"The birds upon the treetops sing their song,
The angels chant their chorus all day long,
The flowers in the garden blend their hue,
So why shouldn't I, why shouldn't you praise Him too?
Why shouldn't I, why shouldn't you praise Him too?"

FROM "THE BIRDS UPON THE TREETOP" CHILDREN'S HYMN

I love birdsong. When the spring peepers are out and the birds awake before dawn, it is like music to my ears because it holds the promise of spring, warmer weather, and new growth. I love this musical invitation to a new season. Yet, there are times when the birdsong sounds more like an alarm clock than a beautiful chorus. When the window is open and the sun has not quite risen, and the birds are busy building a nest right outside my bedroom, it can be annoying!

I remember one of those "annoying" mornings, when we visited friends in Abbotsford, B.C. We were there to attend a conference focused on prayer, and how a complaining and "victim mentality"* can affect how we pray. The truth we received at that conference became one of the core teachings of my life. One of my "aha" moments was the awareness that I lived inside that victim mentality to the detriment of my relationships and my walk with God. So here I was, learning this good content for life transformation, and the simplest of circumstances exposes me. With a three-hour time change, we were feeling a bit jet-lagged and were hoping for as much sleep as possible. Early one morning, hours before the conference began, we woke up to the beautiful song of robins outside our open window. I was so annoyed, I started muttering and complaining as I got up to close the window. I was feeling sorry for myself as a victim of the birds, the open window, and the spring. But before I crawled back into bed, I caught myself. I was doing the very thing that would draw me away from God's abundant, beautiful heart by complaining and feeling sorry for myself. Yikes! I was cut to the heart. It was so powerful an awareness that I have never forgotten it. Once that "victim awareness" set in, I started to give thanks. I thanked God that I could be at the conference. I thanked Him for what I was learning. I thanked Him for exposing my heart that wanted sleep more than Him. I thanked Him for the birds. I thanked Him for the window and our friend's hospitality. I can't remember if I fell back to sleep, but today it doesn't matter. I am just so glad Jesus showed me my heart that morning. It is a continuous reminder that gratitude shapes me into a woman after God's heart.

> THIS DOESN'T MEAN GOD WON'T GIVE YOU MORE THAN YOU CAN HANDLE, BUT IT DOES MEAN THAT HE WILL PROVIDE FOR YOU, AND MAKE A "WAY OF ESCAPE" FOR YOU WHEN YOU ARE TEMPTED TO COMPLAIN.

There is a lot to learn from God's Word about the effects of complaining. The story of the Israelites' journey through the wilderness found in the book of Exodus is a great warning to us about the perils of complaining. You could say that some of their complaining got them stuck wandering around for 40 years, keeping them from the Promised Land. In Exodus 16, the people complained against Moses and Aaron in the wilderness: "Oh that we had died by the hand of the Lord in the land of Egypt, when we sat by the pots of meat and when we ate bread to the full! For you have brought us out into this wilderness to kill this whole assembly with hunger" (Exodus 16:2-3, NKJV).

They complained about the food, so God gave them manna and meat to eat. What is interesting to me is that while they said their complaint was against Moses and Aaron, it was really against the Lord. Moses said, "This shall be seen when the Lord gives you meat to eat in the evening, and in the morning bread to the full; for the Lord hears your complaints which you make against Him. And what are we? Your complaints are not against us but against the Lord" (Exodus 16:8, NKJV).

"Your complaints aren't against us, but against the Lord."

I don't usually think of it this way. When I complain I may know *what* I am complaining about, but I haven't thought about *who* I am complaining against. I find that I might be guilty of the very thing the Israelites were found guilty of—complaining against the Lord. As I sit here and consider the tone and nature of my complaints, I recognize that I suffer the same ailment of complaint against the Lord that Israel suffered. Perhaps I question His goodness because He won't make my life easier by changing my circumstances. Or He won't give me more money, or make my marriage better, or intervene in healing my dying friend. Do I, then, trust the One whom the Bible says is so trustworthy?

In the end, God answered the complaint of the Israelite people as He is often seen doing. He answers. He gave them manna. He gave them water. He provided for them in hard places, though perhaps Israel could not see clearly that it was provision.

These are not easy thoughts, ideas, or questions. I wonder if you thought you would stumble upon them when you opened this book about trust, worry, and freedom. You might be feeling like you can't go any further, so you are about to shut the book. Yet, I think we need to venture here. Am I blaming God? Are you blaming God? Is our complaint against the Lord? And is my worry over finances really a camouflage for my complaint that God isn't intervening the way I want Him to?

God warns in the New Testament about having complaining hearts. Philippians 2:14 says, "Do all things without complaining and disputing that you may become blameless and harmless, children of God without fault in the midst of a crooked and perverse generation, among whom you shine as lights in the world" (NKJV). 1 Corinthians 10 speaks to us also of complaint: "And do not become idolaters...nor let us tempt

Christ, as some of them also tempted, and were destroyed by serpents, nor complain, as some of them also complained, and were destroyed by the destroyer" (10:7, 9-10). It goes further to say that these examples are written for our admonition so that we understand we are susceptible to fall just as Israel did. "Therefore let him who thinks he stands take heed lest he fall. No temptation has overtaken you except such as is common to man; but God is faithful who will not allow you to be tempted beyond what you are able, but with the temptation will also make the way of escape, that you may be able to bear it" (10:12-13).

This doesn't mean God won't give you more than you can handle, but it does mean that He will provide for you and make a "way of escape" for you when you are tempted to complain. How does He do this? He does this by providing the vehicle of gratitude. Let's go back to my bird story. I became aware of my early morning complaints and, once aware, I intentionally adjusted into humble thankfulness. God encourages us in 1 Thessalonians 5:18 that "in everything give thanks for this is the will of God in Christ Jesus concerning you" (NKJV). In everything. Instead of complaining, give thanks. In everything, offer earnest and humble prayers with thanksgiving—this is the way of escape from worry offered in Philippians 4. In exchange, we receive Christ's peace: a peace that passes understanding; a peace that doesn't fix but abides in us as God's daughters and sons. It is a peace that flows from abiding in Him.

MEDITATE: 1 THESSALONIANS 5:18, 1 CORINTHIANS 10:1-13

CULTIVATING COMMUNION
Let's take three steps together today as we look at worry in light of a complaining mindset.

1. Is your worry a camouflage for your complaint that God isn't as trustworthy as you think He should be? Or perhaps your worry isn't a complaint against God, but you are complaining. Ask yourself and His Spirit what might be at the root of this struggle right now. Wait before the Lord as you reflect on this.

2. Next, take some time to confess anything that might be coming to mind. Remember that repentance is a complete turn around from the way we are going and provides a means of refreshing in our walk with God (see Acts 3:19).

Here is a simple format for confession:

Heavenly Father, I confess *(name the sin)* as my sin. I repent of it and I ask you to forgive me. As I confess my sin in the name of your Son Jesus, I know I am cut free from the attachments to *(name the sin)* and the influences that hinder and entangle me in that sin. God's Word promises that if we confess our sins, He is faithful and just to forgive us our sins and purify us from all unrighteousness. Today, I receive your forgiveness and thank you, Jesus. Cleanse me, Jesus, by your blood. Thank you so much for all You are and all You offer to me."

3. Now express your gratitude and thanksgiving. Ask God to grant you a thankful heart. Get in the habit of writing down your thanks, or saying it aloud to your friends or family.

*A victim mentality refers to a mentality that acts out of woundedness. I don't refer here to true victims of crimes, violence, or abuse. This reference is for people who feel sorry for themselves because of their circumstances. A person with this victim mindset can be bound by fear and complaining, as well as feel defensive. In this mindset, a person can overreact to people and situations they can't control. They expect others to make them happy. This person can respond by manipulating others out of anger and self-pity. (This definition came from the conference we attended.)

Lament

"Lament is part of being human. It's the gathering up of our pain, our disappointments, our confusion, and with that gathering up, it is bringing that expression to God. I think that is part of what is inherent in the word lament. It is our pain, but it is where that pain is directed. I think God already knows the condition of our lives, and of our hearts, but He is like a good father who wants us to trust Him enough to share it."

BRIAN DOERKSEN, CANADIAN WORSHIP ARTIST

Up to this point, we have stretched our understanding of how to rejoice in the Lord when worry overwhelms us. We have learned how gratitude positively reshapes our perceptions, so that instead of complaining, we give thanks for all we have been given even in the midst of difficulties and setbacks. With an understanding of rejoicing and gratitude as guides on our journey, I want to introduce another tool that at first may feel like complaining.

We find a beautiful liturgical practice in the Psalms that will help us express our worry and anxiety in a way that God Himself has provided for us. It is called lament. This is not just complaining to ourselves or our friends about our sorrows. This is bringing our pain to God. So often, I get mired in my complaints because I haven't brought them to Jesus—which is the whole point of lament.

In Psalm 13, we find a great example of lament as the shepherd-king David expresses his cries to God over the victory of his enemies:

How long, Lord? Will you forget me forever? How long will you hide your face from me? How long must I wrestle with my thoughts and day after day have sorrow in my heart? How long will my enemy triumph over me? Look on me and answer, Lord my God. Give light to my eyes, or I will sleep in death, and my enemy will say, "I have overcome him," and my foes will rejoice when I fall (Psalm 13:1-4, NIV).

Canadian writer, worship leader, and song artist, Brian Doerksen has put these words to music in the song, "Psalm 13 (How Long O Lord)."[1] It is from Brian's music and teaching, alongside the Psalms of David, that I have learned so much about lament. Many years ago, as I was just beginning to learn, reflect and understand the need for lament, both personally and corporately, my brother Jamie died in a car accident. I remember sitting in our church soon after he died. The worship music that morning was about the greatness of God, how His joy is our strength, and what a great God we serve. These facts about God are true but, that morning, there was so much grief in my heart, and I had no way to express it. I yearned for an expression of that grief in the midst of the congregation. I looked but could not find one. What I found instead were words of celebration—rise, rejoice, and sing!

Please don't misunderstand me. I have been that worship leader who tries to "rally the troops" into praise and thanksgiving. There is definitely a time and place for all of these good things as we have already been learning. However, there was something missing for me. What I began to understand and discover was that, in the church tradition I was a part of, there was no place for lament as part of that expression of gratitude and praise. I also started to realize that I was not alone. Many people were struggling, but had no safe place within the Body of Christ to express their sorrows, their struggles, or their tears. I was hungering for a place where I could rejoice with those who rejoice, but also weep with those who weep.

So what exactly is lament? Isn't this just a fancy word for complaining?

Doerksen says, lament is our pain gathered up and brought to God. It is in the bringing of our pain to God—the One who can make a difference and bring about change—that makes lament what it is:

> Lament is part of being human. It's the gathering up of our pain, our disappointments, our confusion, and with that gathering up, it is bringing that expression to God. I think that is part of what is inherent in the word lament. It is our pain, but it is where that pain is directed. I think God already knows the condition of our lives, and of our hearts, but He is like a good father who wants us to trust Him enough to share it. What lament is in essence for me is our pain, where we gather it up and we bring it to the One who already knows, but is longing for us to be that covenant partner with Him. We aren't just the yes man or yes woman that says we will show up when we are ready to praise but when we are in pain we stay away. We are in a relationship [where] we can bring our pain as well.[2]

> MANY PEOPLE WERE STRUGGLING, BUT HAD NO SAFE PLACE WITHIN THE BODY OF CHRIST TO EXPRESS THEIR SORROWS, THEIR STRUGGLES, OR THEIR TEARS. I WAS HUNGERING FOR A PLACE WHERE I COULD REJOICE WITH THOSE WHO REJOICE, BUT ALSO WEEP WITH THOSE WHO WEEP.

Lament is more than singing blues music, complaining, or staying in the pit together. From my own experience in expressing worry, sorrow, or grief to God, once lament is poured out, it is there I can find the breakthrough of praise and thanksgiving and the place of deeper trust. This is true of Psalm 13. We can find shepherd-king David breaking through into praise as he writes: "But I trust in your unfailing love; my heart rejoices in your salvation. I will sing the Lord's praise, for he has been good to me" (Psalm 13:5-6, NIV).

Scholar and writer Soong-Chan Rah writes about the need for lament in the American evangelical church. In his book—a study of Lamentations—called *Prophetic Lament, A Call for Justice in Troubled Times*, Rah identifies the inequality of what he calls the "theology of celebration" with our need for lament. "To only have a theology of celebration at the cost of the theology of suffering is incomplete. The intersection of the two threads provides the opportunity to engage in the fullness of the gospel message. Lament and praise must go hand in hand."[3]

If lament is gathering our pain and bringing it to God, and if lament brings us to a deeper place of trust in His unfailing love where we, then, offer sacrifices of praise to God, perhaps it can help us on our journey from worry over finances to trust in His care and provision. This is a place where we can engage in the fullness of the gospel as lament and praise walk hand-in-hand.

MEDITATE: PSALM 13

CULTIVATING COMMUNION
Have you ever considered lament? What are your inhibitions about expressing your sorrows to God? How do you think lament can help you in your worries and bring you to closer trust in God? Do you think lament will help you trust God more?

Write down your thoughts. Consider. Ponder. Write. Pray. Remember, lament isn't a place we pitch our tents. It is a place where the pain and despair flow through us to Him. End your time by listening to Brian Doerksen's song called "Psalm 13." You can find it on YouTube.

SIDE BAR:

Complaining and Lament

Complaining is the expression of our dissatisfaction or annoyance with something or someone. Complaint wants commiseration. It looks for a place to express itself so that people can share in that dissatisfaction. Complaint, however, doesn't go to the source of the complaint. It is a surface-level expression that may not want a resolution. Complaints want to be heard and stroked and recognized but will leave people in misery. Complaints may not make sense either because the true sorrow or source is not understood or recognized.

Lament is the gathering up of pain, sorrows and grief, offering and expressing them directly to God, sometimes through others and with others. Lament wants validation. Lament wants affirmation that the sorrows are valid and worthwhile. Lament is expressed as often as needed and is not stagnant. It flows out of the source of pain and gives way to a deep understanding of the cause of the grief and suffering. Lament allows people to face the pain, sit with the pain, and attend to the pain by pouring it out. It is a deeper level expression than complaint. It is an important part of our relationship with the Lord as it leads us, in honesty, to the comforting heart of God. Lament is the place where we are seen, where God responds, and our sorrow is turned into trusting praise.

Cries of the Heart

"All my longings lie open before you, Lord;
my sighing is not hidden from you.
My heart pounds, my strength fails me;
even the light has gone from my eyes.
My friends and companions avoid me because of my wounds;
my neighbors stay far away."

PSALM 38:9-11 (NIV)

Let's be honest and continue our discussion on the gift of lament.

So often, I hear the stories of Christ-followers who are unable to be honest with God about their pain, sorrow, and grief. Somehow we grow up thinking that complaining and "cries of the heart" are all the same, and we keep the griefs hidden within our hearts and minds. These sorrows then seep out in other ways that aren't healthy for our bodies, minds, or emotions. They can become sources of bitterness, anger, and even violence. Or they become the foundation stones for "limiting beliefs" about who God is and who we are in relation to Him.

Scripture is clear that we are not to complain. However, God's Word also leaves us clear examples of lamentation. In fact, there is a whole book in the Old Testament—Lamentations—devoted to the cries and suffering of the people of God over the loss of Jerusalem by the Babylonians in 587 BCE.

The story of Hagar and Ishmael in the Wilderness of Beersheba is also a story of sorrow and lament, but hope as well. Cast out by his father Abraham, Ishmael and his mother are left to die in the wilderness. The water runs out so Hagar places the boy under a shrub and walks away. She cannot bear to see him die. "Let me not see the death of the boy," she says. So she sits opposite him, lifts her voice, and weeps. In fact, the New King James Version says she was sobbing (see Genesis 21:16). In this moment, God takes notice. He hears Ishmael's voice, and Scripture says that the Angel of God calls to Hagar out of heaven and asks: "'What ails you Hagar?' Fear not, for God has heard the voice of the lad where he is. Arise, lift up the lad and hold him with your hand, for I will make him a great nation" (Genesis 21:17-18, NKJV).

> SO OFTEN, I HEAR THE STORIES OF CHRIST-FOLLOWERS WHO ARE UNABLE TO BE HONEST WITH GOD ABOUT THEIR PAIN, SORROW, AND GRIEF. SOMEHOW WE GROW UP THINKING THAT COMPLAINING AND "CRIES OF THE HEART" ARE ALL THE SAME, AND WE KEEP THE GRIEFS HIDDEN WITHIN OUR HEARTS AND MINDS.

Ishmael and Hagar are seen. Ishmael has a promise as the seed of Abraham, and God has promised to bless that seed. Their lament is heard and God responds to them. "Then God opened her eyes, and she saw a well of water. And she went and filled the skin with water and gave the lad a drink" (Genesis 21:19, NKJV).

God opened her eyes.

This wasn't the first time she saw God's hand of provision. In her pregnancy, Hagar fled to the wilderness from Sarai and Abram because of Sarai's harshness. The Angel of the Lord found her by a spring of water and asks, "Where have you come from, and where are you going?"

She answers, and God's response to her is one of direction, provision, and promise:
- "Return to your mistress, and submit yourself under her hand."
- "I will multiply your descendants exceedingly, so they shall not be counted for multitude."
- "Behold, you are with child, and you shall bear a son. You shall call his name Ishmael, because the Lord has heard your

affliction" (see Genesis 16:9-11, NKJV).

The Lord hears her affliction and, in that moment, Hagar understands and calls the name of the Lord who spoke to her, "the-God-Who-Sees" (see Genesis 16:13). God has come to Hagar in both stories and asks her what is troubling her, and what she is doing. He wants to hear her response even though He knows. God comes with the same questions to us today. Can you hear Him asking you?

- What ails you?
- Where have you come from?
- Where are you going?

He is the God-Who-Sees. He didn't take Hagar out from under Sarai's roof. He sent her back. He doesn't always take us out of the situation we are lamenting, but He provides for us in it. He has promises for each of us if we will lament and listen to His response.

MEDITATE: GENESIS 16, GENESIS 21:1-21, PSALM 30

CULTIVATING COMMUNION

What ails you?
Where have you come from?
Where are you going?

Consider one of these questions in your time with God today. Write out the question in your journal or take the question out for a walk with you. If you are suffering, grieving, or despairing in your heart, start to express that to the Lord. Go back to Psalm 13 and write it out as your own prayer of lament, but add your own questions and your own praise at the end.

Perhaps you aren't in a season of grief or loss. Reflect on how God has brought you through times of suffering, and pray or write a prayer of thanksgiving and gratitude. Take Psalm 30 and pray it as your own prayer of reflection and praise.

"Weeping may endure for a night, but rejoicing comes in the morning" (Psalm 30:5b, NKJV).

The Importance of Community

Five years after our wedding, we moved to a small community for my managerial job which meant my husband, Brian, was back to working entry level jobs. A year later, we joyfully welcomed our first child and, as Brian took paternity leave, I returned to my job. After attempting to juggle a challenging schedule, we prayerfully sought God's direction as we looked towards our years of family life. We felt strongly that I should stay at home with our kids and trust in God's providence as we made that choice. Little did we know!

The next seven years we were blessed with three beautiful daughters and some very difficult financial years. We fondly refer to them as our "seven lean years of Biblical proportion" :-)! It was during these financially challenging times that we both felt and saw the loving hand of God's provision, sometimes knowing where the support came from and sometimes not. We did all we could to live as frugally as possible while staying committed to tithing on what money came in.

We belonged to the local Presbyterian church which had a heart for people. The young moms there supported each other with meals or practical help when someone was sick or had a baby. We had a very old car with faulty locks—everyone knew it! Not infrequently, we would discover a bag of groceries on the front seat after returning from errands, always exactly what we needed! Another significant provision came through two couples in our church when they paid our mortgage one month. We learned a lot through this gift, which saw us over the hump of a few difficult months and allowed us to keep our house. Another instance was when Brian received a Christmas bonus which was the exact amount to pay for the muffler that had to be replaced. These are but a few of the many stories of how God miraculously saw us through these times. We look back on them in awe and wonder at the hand of God's care throughout those years. Not to say we didn't have tough moments, but we had encouraging friends, the verses in Matthew 6:25-34, and "my song," "Great is

Thy Faithfulness," to carry us through.

Since those days, as life became more stable, we have been able to "pay it forward." We have found ourselves in a position to bless others in difficult circumstances: by helping with a mortgage, tuition support, and groceries. We partnered with God to encourage others as He has encouraged us. We also learned a lot about ourselves, about community, and about our loving Heavenly Father. We have learned to take all our money decisions to God, to receive God's blessings and gifts with humility, and to be more and more attentive to the voice of the Holy Spirit as He whispers and nudges us to share and support the community around us.

PAULINE WEBB
HUNTSVILLE, ONTARIO, 2021

The Sweater

Linger with what provokes you. I want to put those words on a t-shirt. I need to remind myself again and again, that when irritation or disappointment rises inside of me, there is usually an issue God is bringing to my attention; it's usually a "me" issue, not God's or anyone else's.

Many years ago, before we had kids, David made a request of me that brought me face-to-face with my selfishness. I was irritated and disappointed with his whole idea. He asked me to give something away that felt too hard to give. It was a situation where I knew the "good" thing to do, but I didn't want to do it. I didn't know the "linger with what provokes you" phrase but, linger I did.

Let me tell you the story.

I am an amateur, intermediate knitter. I don't tackle projects that are too tough or intricate. I enjoy knitting for meditative purposes and relaxation. Right now, knitting socks and crocheting shell blankets are my favourite projects.

All those years ago, before our oldest daughter was born, I was working on a thick, warm, deep blue sweater for David. It was the first time I had tackled a sweater project of this nature; basically straight knitting but, for a first sweater it was challenging enough. I don't remember how long it took me to finish, but I do remember the elation I felt when it was done. When I brought it to David, he was grateful and proud. We were both amazed I had stuck with it—and finished!

It was just a matter of moments, however, for David's generous heart and mind to form an idea: he wanted to give the sweater away!

I was stunned; maybe a little hurt. Then, he told me why. A new friend was going to Russia for four months to do mission work. She didn't have a lot of warm clothing or money. "Wouldn't it be nice to give her this warm sweater as she heads out into the cold?"

I told him I needed three days. I was going to linger with what was provoking me. I was irritated and disappointed with his request. Somehow I knew this was what God wanted, but I didn't want to do it, and I needed to understand why my heart was so resistant to this generosity.

Why did this request bother me so much? Looking back on it, there were a few things:

- I was close-fisted. I had worked hard on this project. It was a gift for David. I wouldn't likely ever make him a sweater again. Really, I was coming face-to-face with my selfishness. I knew this was what God wanted, but I simply didn't want to obey.
- I was irritated because this request was not part of my plan. It may sound funny to you, but I think I was afraid of letting go. I was living in my own smallness, not God's wider, bigger plan.
- I was also worried. My fears about giving to others are often wrapped up in my worry that I won't have enough in the future. This situation was no different: not enough money to buy more yarn, not enough time to knit another sweater. My resistance to generosity is often based in my fear that I won't have enough tomorrow.

Essentially, my wrestling throughout those three days showed me that I was worried about me. It was all about me: my control, my fears, my selfishness. Lingering and wrestling with these thoughts and attitudes was sobering. Who was I trusting anyway? I was resistant to change and God's generous heart because it was inconveniencing me. I wasn't thinking of meeting a need in someone else's life, I was thinking about myself.

Does any of this sound familiar to you? Have you ever lingered or wrestled through these same issues? Have your plans ever been derailed by God's? How have you responded? Have you simply ignored His voice? Or have you lingered with Him in the discomfort of His request?

As I uncovered my selfish attitude, I began to understand I was living according to my own small story. It was like I had been invited to a feast table of delicacies and scrumptious food, but I was bringing my own bread and water, and I wouldn't even share that. Like a woman who is afraid of the future, I was hovering and protecting these small bits of food when all around me I had only to open myself up to the table of the Lord; a table that offers abundant provision for all who come. I could offer Him the bread and water I was bringing and, in exchange, He would meet all my needs.

I may not have understood all of these insights at the time but, today, they unfold before me as I linger and remember. My clenched fist—of selfishness and fear that I would not have enough for tomorrow—was controlling and killing the abundant life promised to me in Christ. I was not allowing the generosity of Christ to free me because I was focused on myself and my own small story. This small living did not do me well then and, I knew if I continued in it, would only strangle out the promises of God in my life for the future, keeping me from the purposes of the Kingdom of God and from experiencing abundant intimacy with Him.

So what happened at the end of those three "lingering" days? We gave our friend the sweater. There is so much more to this story, but one beautiful lesson was my discovery that, with God, giving is a profound and beautiful privilege. God was so patient with me as I started to trust His heart in giving, in showing me He wanted me part of a greater plan. It is always a greater story than simply hoarding something not meant for me.

Eventually, over a decade later, David did get another homemade sweater. It's deep hunter green in colour and as warm and cozy as you can get! Those are the only two sweaters I have ever made.

MEDITATE: *2 Corinthians 9:6-11*

CULTIVATING COMMUNION

What is your response after reading this chapter? Can you relate to being irritated by something or someone? Do you linger there to discover what is going on in your mind and heart?

This book is about cultivating trust with God. It is also about looking at your worries and fears around finance and your future. So today, let's ask ourselves the questions around worry about money and dare to linger there. Embracing the wisdom from *Sensible Shoes,* "learn to linger with what provokes you. You may just find the Spirit of God moving there."[1]

Consider:
1. What is keeping you up at night?
2. Take a moment and ask the Lord why this is troubling you? It may take moments, or perhaps even days, to discover what is the true source of the worry or anxiety. For instance, your worry may be based on a past story or circumstance that caused you stress, and you don't want to live through that again. Or, like me, perhaps fear of not having enough in the future is creating the anxiety.
3. Whatever you discover about what is keeping you up at night, ask God for help. Ask Him to show you what beliefs you have that are limiting your trust in Him in this specific situation.

Tell God that you want to walk in the freedom of trust going forward in the situation. And keep talking to Him about it.

For example:
1. **What is keeping me up at night?** I am worried that, if we give money to our church community this month, we won't have enough to make our car payment.
2. **Lord, why is this troubling me so much?** I think I am focusing on the wrong thing. I am seeing all the bills that are piling up, but I am not looking at what I have in the gifts of my home, my family, my friends, and my relationship with Christ. I am focused on the lack and not the plenty.
3. **God, what belief do I have that is part of this worry?** I am sensing that at the core I don't believe God will take care of me, so I want to go back to Psalm 23 and understand that the Lord is my Shepherd who takes care of all my needs. I also will give to our church this month even though I feel anxious. I will ask God to help me walk this out.

It's Not Mine

"After the faith decision, all else is stewardship."
LORNE W. JACKSON, PRESIDENT, CANADIAN NATIONAL CHRISTIAN FOUNDATION

"Mine. Mine. Mine!"

Those are words I heard from my toddlers when they fought over toys. They were on the threshold of learning—learning they weren't the centre of the universe. Sharing was a thing, and the toys did not belong only to them. I am sure you can relate. How hard is it for us to "give away" our hard-earned cash or to share what we have? Remember "the sweater" story? I had to learn to give the sweater, but behind that lesson was something I didn't recognize at the time: God was asking me to steward something that was never mine in the first place.

Never mine.

The sweater.
The ability to knit.
The money to buy the yarn.

Never mine.

Knowing that I am a created being, not the Creator, has been a wonderful starting point for me in releasing what I have—understanding God owns it all, and not I. Scripture says, "the earth is the Lord's, and everything in it, the world, and all who live in it; for he founded it on the seas and established it on the waters" (Psalm 24:1-2 NIV). Isaiah 45:5-7 declares who God is: "I am the Lord, and there is no other; there is no God besides Me. I will gird you, though you have not known Me, that they may know from the rising of the sun to its setting that there is none besides Me. I am the Lord, and there is no other" (NKJV).

In my financial journey of letting go of worry, I continue to remind myself that what I have isn't mine. All I am and have has been given as a gift for me to manage and steward. It is important for me to know it belongs to the Lord, Yahweh—my Creator. As I surrender to God all that I am, I also want to learn that the One who owns it all is trustworthy, loving, good, holy, and just. I want to know as Moses and Abraham, David and Samuel, John the Baptist and the Apostle Paul, that God is who He says He is and that He is good. Though I may not understand why I stand where I am—perhaps struggling to live on less than I make, or struggling through job loss, or a health problem—I can trust He will lead me through and He will turn it all to my good, if only to draw me closer to Him and His heart. He is my God. He is jealous for me. He will not share His glory with another. He wants all of me, not just parts. I cannot serve two masters. Serving mammon keeps me away from the One who loves me and died for me. When I don't surrender and understand my position as His daughter and His steward, I will be choosing mammon's ways by default. My surrender to God daily needs to be intentional.

What if you don't know that He is good? What if you have lost hope in His promises? What if worries have darkened your eyes, and you are feeling like you cannot break through to understand that the great Owner of it all is good and loving, and is the Shepherd who leaves the 99 to come and find you (see Luke 15:4)?

There are no easy answers. Yet, even in the discomfort of finding our way out of worry and into deeper trust, we know God is with us and His beautiful Holy Spirit will lead the way. Jesus tells us in John 15 how important it is to abide in Him, to rest in Him, and to pursue relationship with Him. Jesus is the vine. We are the branches. This is what He tells us:

He who abides in Me, and I in him, bears much fruit; for without Me you can do nothing. If anyone does not abide in Me, he is cast out as a branch and is withered; and they gather them and throw them into the fire, and they are burned. If you abide in Me, and My words abide in you, you will ask what you desire, and it shall be done for you. By this My Father is glorified that you may bear much fruit; so you will be My disciples (vs. 5-8, NKJV).

So this is my heartfelt encouragement to you—don't abandon God. Turn back to Him. Start learning who He is by spending time reading His Word. If you don't like to read, listen to His words. Pray. Journal. Just talk to Him. Go for walks. There are so many ways to connect with Him, and He is longing to capture your attention. As you grow in your understanding of Him, you will be able to trust His heart for you and, as a result, you will be able to release your worries to Him more and more.

MEDITATE: ISAIAH 43:10

CULTIVATING COMMUNION

Remember, you are a gift. Your breath is a gift. He pours out His gifts over you daily. Today, I want you to go back to your list of God's qualities that we learned about in the chapter "Throwing Glitter."[1] Choose another quality about God that you have trouble believing. Get on the internet and do a biblical word search and find the Scriptures that speak of these qualities. Make notes. Write down one verse that speaks to that quality and paste it on your bathroom mirror or have it on your nightstand. Learn the verse. When you are tempted to worry over finances, go back to that verse and truth and repeat it to yourself. This is a practical way of setting your eyes on Him.

God is:

Good	Wise	Glorious
Powerful	Holy	Righteous
Great	Merciful	Just
Excellent	Changeless	Full of Grace
Full of Love	Almighty	Sinless

All-Knowing	Faithful	Worthy
True	Radiant	All-Sufficient
Pure	Magnificent	Light of the World

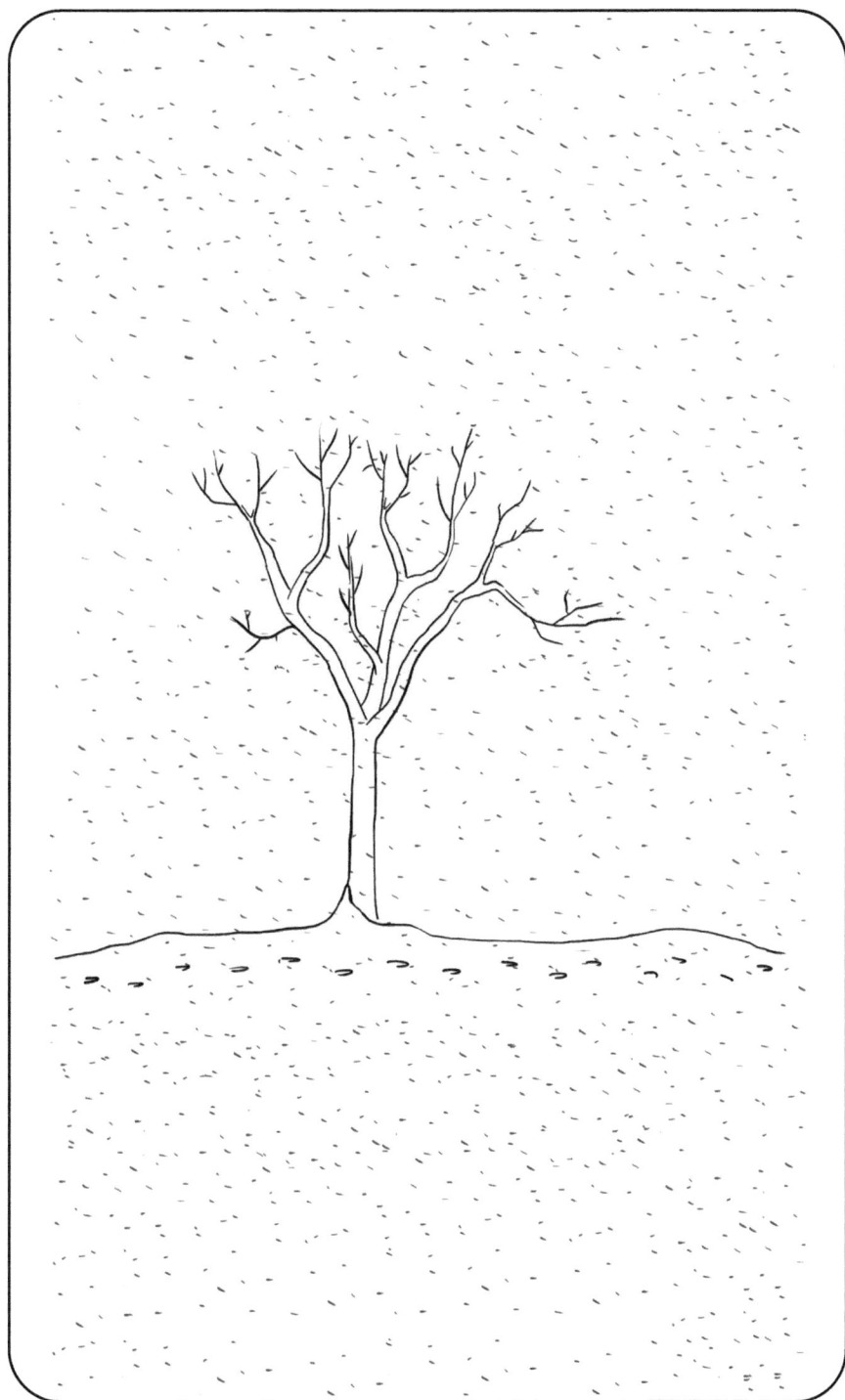

SIDE BAR:

Stewardship

"If you ignore the fact that God is the source of everything and make a converted and sanctified self the source, it is just as bad as it can be because final trust in God has been taken away. Self judges God and man, and holds God to be less than He is and man to be more than he is. This is our trouble."

A.W. TOZER, PASTOR AND AUTHOR, FROM *THE CRUCIFIED LIFE*

Let's take a look at stewardship in another way, through one of my husband David's childhood stories. As stewards we can gain more understanding of God's heart for us, and release the worry about finances that often restrains us.

When I was a young boy, we lived in smalltown Eastern Ontario where I could use my bicycle to get anywhere I needed to go. My parents were seldom worried about my personal safety—literally half of the village knew our family and, if I ever needed something, help was not far off. As a young man with a bicycle, my mom would regularly give me money to go to the store and buy groceries. It was often something she had forgotten to buy earlier that week. I would take the money, bike to the store, give the money to the store owner, and then jump back on my bike and deliver the goods to my mother in record time.

I never questioned the purpose of the money. It was clear from the start that this was Mom's money, that she wanted that money to advance her objective of caring for our family, and that she needed my help to do it. I was the steward of both the money and the responsibility. I cannot ever remember questioning my mother and asking her if she really needed me to run the errand: "Mom, do you really need me to get lard? Would butter not be better?" And I never thought of questioning her timing: "Do you need this right now? I am busy. Let me see if I can fit you in next week."

Stewardship starts with childlike faith and obedience. When David went to get the groceries for his mother, he did not stop and analyse her request or his response, he simply went and did as she asked.

David notes: *When we get older there is a temptation to take ownership: to question, to pause, to take the credit, to feel proud about helping. But that is flawed thinking even though it is a normal, fleshly response. Jesus tells us to become like little children in His Kingdom (see Matthew 18). I think this is one of the ways He was talking about. Every time you get a pay cheque, it is like God is sitting down with you directing you how to use what He has given. "David, you have worked and laboured for the money I have given you this week. With it you will get your groceries, pay the hydro bill, give some to the work I am doing at church, and this week I have a special surprise for someone, and I want you to share what you have with them."*

In this journey with God, we have choices before us. We choose to believe we are either owners or stewards. We choose to ask God what to do with His money, or we make our own decisions. We choose to obey His voice—or not. We choose to focus on our money worries, or we choose to trust Him. Knowing who He is, and knowing we are stewards, ushers us into freedom. We are released from worry because we know the owner, we know the heart of the owner, and we know the owner is good.

Seek My Heart

"Therefore I am now going to allure her; I will lead her into the wilderness and speak tenderly to her. There I will give her back her vineyards, and will make the Valley of Achor a door of hope. There she will respond as in the days of her youth, as in the day she came up out of Egypt. 'In that day,' declares the Lord, 'you will call me "my husband"; you will no longer call me "my master" ... I will betroth you to me forever; I will betroth you in righteousness and justice, in love and compassion. I will betroth you in faithfulness, and you will acknowledge the Lord.'"

HOSEA 2:14-16 & 19-20 (NIV)

Seek My heart, not My hand. Those words in 2017 would direct and navigate us through one of the most challenging seasons of our marriage and business. We were leaving a prayer retreat with some of our More Than Enough team, where we had been seeking the Lord's direction. David and I had come with questions, insecurities and anxieties about how we were running the business and ministry of MTE. What we were left with was an image of a bullseye in the centre of a target, and the words, "Seek My heart, not My hand."

What did these words mean? We were about to find out. David and I had been praying for months for provision to cover the expenses of the business, but things were not shaping up as we had hoped. We had business debt, salaries to pay, and yet it looked like we didn't have what we needed to do the job. *Were we doing something wrong? Did God hear our prayers? What were we to do next? Would we lose our livelihood or our investment in this calling?*

The prayer retreat came at the perfect time and, after seeking the Lord with our team, we heard God's gentle voice laying down a path for us to follow. David and I needed to pursue His heart of love for ourselves and for those we served. If we didn't, and only called on Him to supply our physical and material needs, we would be missing the mark. It was a serious word and still is. It was an admonishment at a time when we had slipped from simply being in His presence, to pursuing Him because we needed something. As we headed out the doors of that retreat, we were heading into 2018—a year that would be an even tougher year financially.

We went home. David started getting up even earlier to be with the Lord. We returned to the place of waiting, simply being with God, not asking for anything but to know His heart more deeply. It was a time of further surrender and, as bills came that we struggled to pay, I would ask David, "what do we do next?" His response to me that entire year was, "seek His heart, not His hand." Those words continue to ring in my mind.

Hit the bullseye.
Get to the core of what is important.
Seek the heart of God.
Know His heart.

As I think of that time, I am reminded of the Jesus story in Luke 10 where He and His disciples were welcomed into Martha's home. As Martha prepared the meal, Jesus taught, and Martha's sister Mary sat at His feet and listened. Mary was seeking the heart of God. She was seeking life and love—and the words of Christ. Martha was preoccupied with her worries. She needed to provide food for a crowd of people, and she wanted Mary's help. Then, Jesus speaks to Martha. "Martha, Martha," the Lord answered, "you are worried and upset about many things, but few things are needed—or indeed only one. Mary has chosen what is better, and it will not be taken away from her" (Luke 10: 41-42, NIV).

God may have used different words for our circumstances, but I think the heart of what He spoke to us was no different than what He spoke to Martha. "Mary has chosen what is better, and it will not be

THERE MAY BE TIMES FOR CHURNING AND WRESTLING THROUGH ISSUES WITH THE LORD. THERE MAY BE TIMES FOR HEAVY EQUIPMENT WHERE WE FIND SECTIONS OF FALLOW GROUND OF UNBELIEF THAT NEED UPROOTING. HOWEVER, THERE MAY BE TIMES OF WAITING AND LISTENING THAT COME AFTER OR BEFORE THE CHURNING.

taken away from her."

Mary was at Jesus' feet, just as we were attempting to be. We were building, growing, and cultivating faith, love, and trust just as Mary was. We kept going back to His Word to us: "Seek My heart. Seek My heart."

Can you also hear the words of Jesus in Matthew 6: "Seek first God's Kingdom and His righteousness and all these things will be added to you?" Those words are reflected here: "Seek My heart, not My hand. Mary has chosen what is better. It won't be taken from her. Seek Me first."

Now, where does that leave us today? I want to go back to the words of my friend and grain farmer Shelley Spruit. Cultivating trust doesn't mean we are always striving in our growth and churning up the soil. As we have already learned, "no-till" ground preparation and seed planting can be an essential part of farming. As it says in Ecclesiastes, there are times and seasons for everything. Shelley says, "cultivating our relationship with God often means learning to be a Mary instead of a Martha. Waiting, listening, praying are like the realization that 'no-till' with little disturbance of the soil is better than big heavy equipment constantly turning over the soil."

There may be times for churning and wrestling through issues with the Lord. There may be times for heavy equipment, where we find sections of the fallow ground of unbelief that need uprooting. However, there may be times of waiting and listening that come after or before the churning. All of it is preparation, as the seeds of faith, love, and trust grow underground into a strong root system. That was God's direction to us when He said seek *My heart*. Trust, love, surrender, wisdom, and obedience were growing "underground."

In the fall of 2018, as we continued to seek His heart and grow in trust, we received a visitor to our home. This person had been attentive to God, and to us, over the past year and, in a deep gesture of care and love, told us our business debt would be paid in full. This person was going to take the debt and pay for it so we could go about doing God's business without further financial strain. This person was standing in the gap and paying for what we couldn't. We were speechless, amazed, humbled. Our business debt was paid in full that day. While we sought the heart of God, He was taking care of the provision that was too big for us to do on our own.

MEDITATION: LUKE 10:38-42, MATTHEW 6:33, JEREMIAH 17:5-8

CULTIVATING COMMUNION

Perhaps you are in a season of waiting. Perhaps you have been waiting a long time. What word from today speaks to you? In your waiting, are you seeking God's heart for you and the situation you face? Can you identify with Martha perhaps, with her worries and distractions? In a journal, ask the Lord what it looks like for you to seek His heart and not His hand. Wait for His answer. As a picture, memory, or Scripture comes to mind, jot it down and turn it into a prayer of repentance, thanksgiving, or commitment. In this time, visualize God's strong roots of trust growing deep. Look at Jeremiah 17:7-8 (NIV) again. You will never fail to bear fruit if you are growing the roots of trust in God Himself:

> "But blessed is the one who trusts in the Lord,
>   whose confidence is in him.
> They will be like a tree planted by the water
>   that sends out its roots by the stream.
> It does not fear when heat comes;
>   its leaves are always green.
> It has no worries in a year of drought
>   and never fails to bear fruit."

Surrounded

"My Presence will go with you, and I will give you rest."
Spoken by the Lord to Moses in Exodus 33:14 (NIV)

"And Elisha prayed, 'Open his eyes, Lord, so that he may see.'
Then the Lord opened the servant's eyes, and he looked and saw
the hills full of horses and chariots of fire all around Elisha."
2 Kings 6:17 (NIV)

I have spent so much of my last three years listening to the worship song, "Surrounded" (written by Elyssa Smith and recorded by Michael W. Smith)[1]. My kids know I am having some writing time when this song wafts through my work and creative space. I have had to put my earbuds in so I don't drive them crazy! Even this morning, I am listening to it on the back deck of our tiny home; it is a place of birdsong, sunshine, and the reminder that it is in God's presence that I stand, fight, lament, cry out, and pray, relishing the fact that I am His!

"This is how I fight my battles.
It may look like I'm surrounded but I'm surrounded by You."

You see, this week we received news that one of our beloved family members has cancer. In the midst of the pandemic, when so many around us are suffering health and financial crises, this is the cherry on the top of this season's proverbial cake. And yet...

As I weep and cry out to the great Helper of my soul, I am reminded of what David told me at the beginning of the pandemic when people often asked us "Now what?" or "What do we do with our finances now?" David simply said, "He hasn't changed and His Word hasn't

> THIS IS HOW I FIGHT MY BATTLES. I STAND IN PRAISE AND WORSHIP, IN MEDITATION, AND RECOGNITION THAT HE IS GREATER THAN MY CIRCUMSTANCES AND GREATER THAN MY WORRIES ABOUT LIFE, MONEY, OR HEALTH. HE SURROUNDS EACH ONE OF US AND HE SPEAKS TO US CONTINUALLY OF WHO HE IS AND HOW HE LOVES US.

changed. It doesn't change. He asks us to love Him and love others. He asks us to steward what He gives us every single day. His words are true. He is true, and He is good."

David's words are ringing through my ears. It is in God's presence that I find the core, gift, and reward of seeking the kingdom. **He is the gift.** His presence is the anchor. His love is the carrier. His strength is the foundation. His truth is freedom's key. He is good in the midst of cancer, debt, divorce, rebellion, joblessness, worry, and fear. He is good in the midst of victory, favour, long-awaited birth, a new job, and increased wages. Though circumstances change, He remains the good Father, the Father of lights, with whom there is not even a shadow of turning (see James 1:17).

As Hebrews 13:5-6 says, "Let your conduct be without covetousness; be content with such things as you have. For He Himself has said, 'I will never leave you nor forsake you.' So we may boldly say: 'The Lord is my helper; I will not fear. What can man do to me?'"

The Lord
Is
My
Helper.

This is how I fight my battles. I stand in praise and worship, in meditation, and recognition that He is greater than my circumstances and greater than my worries about life, money, or health. He surrounds each one of us and He speaks to us continually of who He is and how He loves us.

This is my urgent message: He is who He says He is and He is trustworthy.

I will say it again: HE IS TRUSTWORTHY. He is who He says He is. He is YHWH—Yahweh. Our very breath. Our life. And HE IS GOOD. HE is the I AM: Redeemer, Deliverer, Saviour, Hope, Comfort, Peace.

I know I have used far too many capital letters to press my point but, like the Apostle Paul, I want to encourage you and urge you: believe that God is who He says He is. Meditate on Him and His truth and grasp who He is, not necessarily who you have perceived Him to be. He is calling us to seek, knock, and ask. When we seek, we will find. That is His promise. We will find the promise of His presence and find out who He is and what He is like. He wants to walk with each of us through all of these circumstances and HE WILL MAKE A WAY. It may not look like the way we had planned, but it will be His way. His goodness, love, and life will surround each of us through it all.

So now we return to where we started. With difficult news like cancer filtering through my life, where am I turning? I want to press in to worship, to praise. I sit here weeping with worry, fear, and grief rising in my heart, but I turn my eyes to Jesus. He accepts my grief, my anxieties, my questions, and my laments about the future. I see His wonderful face and I find His comfort, love, and goodness. He understands. I hear Him whisper to Me: "Trust Me. I have not changed. I am with you. In the worries, the uncertainties, the road ahead, I am here. I will never leave."

In this moment, and in this day, He is enough. I face the road and know I am not alone.

MEDITATE: HEBREWS 13:5,6; ISAIAH 52, 2 KINGS 6:15-23

CULTIVATING COMMUNION

What does it mean for you to be surrounded by God's presence? Take some time to listen to worship and praise music. Sit in the words and music, or go for a walk. As you have been looking at the character qualities of God, take who He is with you into this time. Who is He for your circumstance this morning or evening? What would He speak over you? Write down what you hear. Remember, the Lord is with you. He is mighty to save. The greatest gift of seeking His Kingdom is finding Him and discovering His presence with you. You and I are surrounded by His presence, and in His presence there is rest. Worry often steals our peace and rest, but as we learn to be with Him, to slow down and focus on who He is and His promises to us, we learn to enter that rest more deeply.

Here is an example of taking a financial concern into God's presence:

1. **What does it mean for me to be surrounded by God's presence in my present circumstance?** I am worried about the $2,000 repair bill on my van. My emergency cushion/fund took a hit last month and there isn't enough to cover this expense. But now, I remember that God is bigger than my bill. I remember He created the universe and loves me. He doesn't leave me in my trouble.

2. **In this situation, what quality of God speaks to this circumstance?** He is creative and all-sufficient, and Jesus taught that God knows what I need. I may not see the provision yet, but I am choosing to believe God's Word that He takes care of all my needs. When the answer comes, I also know it may come in a creative way that I haven't imagined.

3. **What do I hear Him saying?** Maybe God is saying, "Pay this bill with the money you have, and I will take care of the future." Maybe He is saying, "Share this situation with a trusted friend." Maybe He is saying, "Just wait and see what I will do." I remind myself of all the creative ways God has surrounded me and answered my prayers in the past. I remind myself that He loves me and has provided for me through many people, in

many situations. And I also remind myself that God wants me to avoid debt because it is a burden and a weight.

4. **End with a prayer of thanks.** As I read the story of 2 Kings 6, I can almost hear the fear in the servant's voice. Yet, I also see the confidence of Elisha. I ask the Lord to open my eyes to see just as Elisha prayed for his servant. "Don't be afraid," the prophet answered. "Those who are with us are more than those who are with them" (2 Kings 6:16, NIV). I thank God that He is opening my understanding and building my trust, and I realize again He hasn't left me alone.

My Unleashed Journey

I had tried for many years to manage my financial affairs, only to find myself deeper in debt with every passing year. Finally, I surrendered to the fact that I needed help.

I could see that my financial situation, if not addressed, would lead me into other addictive behaviours that would only offer temporary relief—and I knew that wasn't God's plan for me. I believed it was His plan for me to overcome this area of my life, through Him and for Him. I also knew it wasn't God's plan for me to declare bankruptcy. I've always believed that if I spent it, I owed it. If I was smart enough to get myself into this mess, I should be smart enough to get myself out.

So, with a heart-stopping amount of debt to clear up, I contacted More Than Enough in October 2019. I knew I'd need to be accountable to someone other than myself, so I elected to enroll in the Unleashed series of workshops and doubled up with one-on-one monthly coaching with the extraordinary Sarah-Jane Ward.

The Unleashed workshops helped give me a new perspective on the role that money has played throughout my life, to my own detriment and to the detriment of those around me. Unleashed provided me with a way to take stock of my own personal short-comings around money and, indeed, my powerlessness to resolve those issues without God's help. It also stirred in me a desire to become a better servant in this area and to help others by sharing my own experience and resources.

CHANGE IN PERCEPTION

Through showing up to the Unleashed sessions, doing the work that was asked, and by following the guidance of my financial coach, my perceptions around money and spending have miraculously started to change. The change in perception is an important piece; without that, my old thinking would continue to take me back into debt. My new perception around money is now more in line with how God would have me think, and shows up in

what He would have me do.

Where once browsing in a shopping mall seemed like a great way to spend an afternoon, now I see it as a waste of time. Not only that, but the better choice seems to be sitting in my backyard spending time in gratitude for the things of God. How did that happen? Unleashed opened a channel through which God's grace could flow.

Thankfully, I am getting closer and closer to being debt free, with God's help and the help of my amazing coach—Sarah-Jane. It was through her direction we were able to put together a realistic picture of where I'm at and what needed to be done to eliminate all debt going forward. She has been an invaluable asset to help me differentiate between the true and the false, and has been unwavering in her commitment to see me set free financially to live a life without debt.

SANDY KINGSTON
OTTAWA, ONTARIO, 2020

Start at the End

"Life is gift, not gain."

DAVID GIBSON, SCHOLAR AND MINISTER, FROM LIVING LIFE BACKWARD: HOW ECCLESIASTES TEACHES US TO LIVE IN LIGHT OF THE END

"I am convinced that only a proper perspective on death provides the true perspective on life. Living in the light of your death will help you to live wisely and freely and generously. It will give you a big heart and open hands, and enable you to relish all the small things of life in deeply profound ways. Death can teach you the meaning of mirth. All this I have learned from Ecclesiastes."

DAVID GIBSON

I was sitting in my mother's living room a few years ago having tea. My mom and I were chatting about life, kids, work, and all those things that fill our time and space. We were also talking about her upcoming move into my sister's home. My Dad died in 2013 and, after living a few years on her own, she decided to move in with my sisters, Mary Anne and Liz. I remember sitting there, looking at the things in the room: the curtains, the floral couch and matching chairs, the television set used more for holding pictures of grandchildren and great-grandchildren than for watching shows, the Trisha Romance painting of Niagara-on-the-Lake where she lived most of her life, and the great grandfather clock that no longer chimed. As I sat with her, a realization came over me: my mother would soon divest herself of these possessions and take only what could fit into one bedroom. All the work over the years, and all the things that filled her home, came down to this moment when she would give it all away.

I realized then that the common phrase about possessions is very true: you really can't take it with you. Our end is death. As much as we try to deny our mortality and try to find ways to extend our lives, we will simply end in the dirt—as dirt. Perhaps I could say it in a nicer way but, no matter how I say it, the reality is the same: the death and decay of our bodies is the end. I realize that as Christ-followers we do have much more hope than that! We may not take anything with us into eternity, but our deaths are more than just decay. We have eternal life as a gift from God as we believe in Christ. We live on!

David Gibson, a minister and scholar from Aberdeen, Scotland says that life is gift, not gain.[1] In his book, *Living Life Backward: How Ecclesiastes Teaches Us To Live In Light Of The End*, he reminds me to keep my moments and my days in perspective: my life on earth is a dot on the timeline of eternity.

Live life in each moment.
Enjoy what God has given as a gift.
Walk each day knowing there is nothing new under the sun.

Ecclesiastes teaches us to live life backward. It encourages us to take the one thing in the future that is certain—our death—and work backward from that point into all the details and decisions and heartaches of our lives and to think about them from the perspective of the end. It is the destination that makes sense of the journey. If we know for sure where we are heading, then we can know for sure what we need to do before we get there. Ecclesiastes invites us to let the end sculpt our priorities and goals, our greatest ambitions and our strongest desires. I want to persuade you that, only if you prepare to die, can you really learn to live.[2]

How does understanding my end help me trust God more deeply and live with less worry about the food I eat, the clothing I wear, and the shelter I need in the here-and-now?

Live life in each moment.
Enjoy what God has given as a gift.
Walk each day knowing there is nothing new under the sun.

Understanding my end, and knowing that worry has been an issue for people since the beginning of our wanderings out of the Garden of Eden, has kept my own struggles and worries in perspective. It may sound funny to you but the words of Ecclesiastes are comforting to me in this regard. They have actually helped me gain immediate perspective on my financial worries when I find myself spiralling.

Live life in each moment.
Enjoy what God has given as a gift.
Walk each day knowing there is nothing new under the sun.

Read Ecclesiastes for yourself. Read Matthew 6 again and consider how much of your life you have spent worrying about money and possessions. Do you really want to spend more of your time worrying about things that may never happen? When you look back on your life, will you see the hours you have devoted to worry or will you see your time spent learning ruthless trust in God?

These are some of Solomon's words:
- "The merest of breath...the merest of breaths. Everything is a mere breath" (1:2)*.
- "A generation goes and a generation comes but the earth remains forever" (1:4).
- "What has been is what will be, and what has been done is what will be done, and there is nothing new under the sun" (1:9).
- "Then I saw that there is more gain in wisdom than in folly, as there is more gain in light than in darkness. The wise person has his eyes in his head, but the fool walks in darkness" (2:13-14).
- "There is nothing better for a person than that he should eat and drink and find enjoyment in his toil. This also, I saw, is from the hand of God, for apart from him who can eat or who can have enjoyment? For to the one who pleases him God has given wisdom and knowledge and joy, but to the sinner he has given the business of gathering and collecting, only to give to

one who pleases God. This also is vanity and a striving after wind" (2:24-26).

- "For everything there is a season, and a time for every matter under heaven" (3:1).
- "He has made everything beautiful in its time. Also he has put eternity into man's heart, yet so that he cannot find out what God has done from the beginning to the end. I perceived that there is nothing better for them than to be joyful and to do good as long as they live; also that everyone should eat and drink and take pleasure in all his toil—this is God's gift to man" (3:11-13).
- "All go to one place. All are from the dust, and to dust all return" (3:20).
- "As you do not know the way the spirit comes to the bones in the womb of a woman with child, so you do not know the work of God who makes everything. In the morning sow your seed, and at evening withhold not your hand, for you do not know which will prosper, this or that, or whether both alike will be good" (11:5-6).

I get this sense as I read Solomon's words and Jesus' words from Matthew 6 that they are speaking together, as if Christ was weaving His words with Solomon's.

Live life in each moment.
Enjoy what God has given as a gift.
Walk each day knowing there is nothing new under the sun.

I know neither Jesus nor Solomon said it exactly like this, but I can hear the two voices together, encouraging us.

- Don't store up for yourselves treasures on earth where moth and rust destroy and where thieves break in and steal; it is all vanity.
- Enjoy your life while living and enjoying God's presence, not striving after folly and earthly possessions, for He makes everything beautiful in its time.

- The time you have is a gift—all your toil and all your work—so think about what you seek in all that work for it is a gift from God's hand.
- Seek His kingdom and His way, otherwise all the striving is in vain.
- The eye is the lamp of the body, and a wise person keeps his eyes in his head. Eyes full of light provide sight for the way ahead. The fool, however, walks in the darkness that comes from within him. When the eyes are dark, how great is that darkness.
- Eat and drink and take pleasure in your toil as if it is God's gift to you, then worry will be kept far from your door.
- Understand the end from the beginning, look at the world around you, and see how God cares and loves as a Father watches over the birds of the sky and the flowers of the field. You are much more valuable.
- Don't worry about tomorrow. God has it all in hand and you don't know how He is going to lay out your tomorrow. Today has enough tasks and considerations so, in the morning, sow your seed and don't withhold doing good in the evening, because you don't know how it is all going to turn out. Keep your head and trust in the One who holds it all. Just remember you don't know the work of God who makes everything, but also remember He knows you and loves you more than you realize.

If God holds everything in His hand, if He loves me like He says, and if there is a season for everything, can I divest myself of worry, just as my mother divested herself of her possessions? Can I dig into the ground of trusting and break up the hard ground of my heart's anxieties, just as my mother, father, sisters, and brothers so often did before planting crops in the ground? Can I dig into trusting God more fully so that the seeds of life, love, joy, and generosity break forth into the fruit of His Kingdom?

Gibson again says:

> Here is wisdom you will not hear anywhere else; take the best of
> what you have and the best of what you are and give them away.
> Hold them out in open hands to God and to others. Worldly wis-
> dom builds bunkers and barns to prepare for disaster. Biblical wis-
> dom instead throws open the windows and doors of our homes and
> builds schools and hospitals and churches, and sees rich Christians
> become much, much poorer than they might otherwise have been.
> Ecclesiastes-type wisdom, Christlike wisdom, grows believers
> who spend their life on living in the world rather than on living in
> the world so as not to die.[3]

As stewards of God's resources we are exchanging money for
something we can't explain—a joy in giving that flows from the
generous DNA of God Himself. This living, this giving, this Kingdom
seeking and trusting, flows out of the joy and pleasure we find in
relationship with Him. This is the Kingdom way. So remember to live
life backward. Learn your end so that you enjoy the journey of living in
the world and not merely living so as not to die. This here-and-now life
is the dot on the long line of eternity. Let's live for the line.

MEDITATE: ECCLESIASTES, MATTHEW 6:19-34

CULTIVATING COMMUNION

Take some time to dig into the book of Ecclesiastes, either by reading
it or listening to it. Then re-read Matthew 6. You could even take time
to read or listen to the entire Sermon on the Mount found in Matthew
5, 6, and 7.

What jumps out at you? Are there any connections God's Spirit is
impressing on your heart between the words of Solomon and Jesus?
What does the Lord want you to do with these truths? Write down what
He is saying to you and take this truth with you into the day. Consider
what this will look like in your life this week. This whole exercise may
take a few days so don't rush through it. Allow God's words and His
Spirit to show you the way.

As it says in the Book of Common Prayer pocket edition, "In our lives, and in our prayers, may Your Kingdom come."

*Gibson explains that our understanding of Ecclesiastes 1:2 may have further nuances that Bible translations have missed.

> I want to propose that many well-intended Bible translations have actually led us astray by translating the Hebrew word **hebel** as "meaningless" in this context. We tend to read this word as if it's spoken by an undergraduate philosophy student who comes home after his first year of studies and confidently announces that the universe as we know it is pointless and life has no meaning. But that is not the Preacher's perspective...In fact, the Hebrew word **hebel** is also accurately translated as "breath" or "breeze." The Preacher is saying that everything is a mist, a vapor, a puff of wind, a bit of smoke.[4]

Going Forward:
LET'S TALK MONEY—TOGETHER

"The church is at an exciting crossroads. We are entering a new day,
new terrain and a new adventure. We are not alone. The Spirit of
God goes before us. The mission of Christ will not fail. A day will
come when the 'kingdom of the world will become the kingdom
of our Lord and of his Messiah, and he will reign forever and ever'
(Revelation 11:15). The next steps are going to be demanding...We
are heading into uncharted territory and are given the charge to
lead a mission where the future is nothing like the past."

*Tod Bolsinger, Vice President, Fuller Theological Seminary, from
Canoeing The Mountains: Christian Leadership in Uncharted Territory*

On our podcast, *Let's Talk Money with Dave and Reb*, we have a tagline
we say every week: "this is a show where we talk about the heart issues
around money." The purpose of the podcast is not only to encourage
people to talk about money, but to get listeners to consider and think
about the heart motivators around money decisions and how they are
tied to their relationship with God.

I don't know how comfortable you are talking about money, but
it really is something that needs to be learned and practised in an
environment that welcomes community and trust. For many of us,
talking about money can feel like getting a tooth pulled without freezing.
There can also be shame, embarrassment, and misunderstanding around
our struggles with money so we won't even try to talk about it. Our
perceptions about how we mismanage our finances can also keep us
in hiding. Then add to that, a religious system that tells us we need to
show up perfectly for God and our Christian community, and talking
about money isn't high on our priority list. The subjects of money,
giving, and stewardship can be minefields in some congregations and

are best left to others, although we aren't quite sure who those "others" are.

It is no wonder, then, that we need to consider the heart issues around money and enter into a dialogue about how to create places of non-judgmental, safe space to have these discussions. Our healing and unity as the body of Christ in the area of finances is dependant on this. Safe conversations in safe spaces, that are honest, challenging, and filled with grace and forgiveness, are the dream of my own heart. Are these spaces possible? If they are, and I believe they are, then we will have the places we need to express our worry and anxiety about our money journeys. We will have the place to confess our sins, failures, and shortcomings, and find forgiveness and a renewed sense of refreshment so we can keep going (see Acts 3:19). I believe that as we get honest with ourselves, in humility, we can start to create the open spaces to have these conversations. We will see ourselves standing on level ground with others. Our struggles, though different in the details, are still struggles that are similar for all of us. We need others as much as they need us. I don't need to have all the answers. You don't need to have all the answers. In fact, it is better if we don't. Our brothers and sisters don't need our answers, they need the Lord's. We can hear the confession and struggles of others—asking good questions and listening well—all the while joining hands in prayer and encouragement, waiting on God and His Word to provide what we need.

Perhaps this is simplistic to say, but I know this is anything but simplistic to carry out. Why do I know this? Because of my own journey as a "recovering judgmentalist." You have no idea how judgmental I can be. A critical nature clothed in pride has not been a helpful companion to me. I am hard on myself—and I am hard on others. Perhaps that is why I am hard on others—because I have had trouble giving grace to myself. The older I get, the more aware I become, and this awareness is a good thing. It helps me keep short accounts with God and others. I am learning to let go of outcomes and receive people just as they are with their whole story, not just what I want their story to be. I know I have hurt others through my judgements and pride, through my "non-listening-know-it-all-ism," but I am learning. By understanding God's love, grace and forgiveness, to and for me, I am growing in giving this love and grace to others. There is hope for me yet!

Hopefully, I am becoming what I have dreamed of becoming: a safe place for others to express their anxieties and fears, and a place that extends hope and love, as people journey with God in their finances. If I can become that space, you can become that space as well. And as we become two spaces, we can become three and four, and ten and twenty. Before you know it, we will create a community space for conversation and growth. We can confess our sins to one another and share our victories. We will grow and be healed together.

Being in a community like this brings financial worry and shortcomings to light. It also dispels the fears and worries because we are carrying the load together. This community becomes a place of victory dances and encouragement as we grow, learn, and succeed together. This is what we need. We don't need to carry these tensions alone. By sharing them in community we become the light set on a hill that Jesus talks about. My husband and financial coach David says,

> One of Satan's greatest powers here on earth is isolation. He did it with Eve in the garden and he does it today in our finances. He tells us we can't share our worries with others, so in our isolation we then continue to struggle. Jesus says let your light shine. As we share our journeys together, the light shines, and others, whom we need, gather together and glorify God in community with us.

"You are the light of the world," Jesus says. "A city that is set on a hill cannot be hidden. Nor do they light a lamp and put it under a basket, but on a lampstand, and it gives light to all who are in the house. Let your light so shine before men, that they may see your good works and glorify your Father in heaven" (Matthew 5:14-16, NKJV).

Just writing about this gets me excited. On the hard days, this is the vision that gets me up in the morning. This is why we work, we talk, and we teach. This is why we walk in community at More Than Enough. This is why we talk about money and the heart issues around money every week on the podcast. The podcast, the workshops, and the coaching we do, are simply vehicles to create and fulfill a vision for something greater than the church has yet experienced in the area of finances. God will bring unity to us in it. This is our hope. This is our freedom.

MEDITATE: MATTHEW 5:14-16, JAMES 5:13-18, ACTS 4:40-47

CULTIVATING COMMUNION

Where do we go from here? How do you and I become a safe place to talk about money, to receive hope and healing, and to create a community united in purpose around our finances? Do you want to become that space, that person?

There is a song written and performed by *FOR KING & COUNTRY*, featuring Kirk Franklin and Tori Kelly, called "Together."[1] It became a theme song for some of us during the pandemic lockdowns of 2020. Take the time to listen or watch the music video. Consider the people in your community and pray this song as a prayer.

I have included three separate Scripture passages today. Take some time over the next few days to pause with these Scriptures. What do they speak to you about building community? What do they speak to you about the hope of being in community? Write down the characteristics of what God's community through us looks like.

Now, after considering these passages, what is the one thing you want to do to become that safe community space for others? Tell a trusted friend or family member what you would like to do to build this kind of *Together* community.[2] Let's become that community together. Let's become a safe place without judgment. Let's become a place of honesty with ourselves, with God, and with others. *Together*.

The Invitation

Here we are at the end.

However.

This ending begins again with God's invitation—His continued invitation for you and me to come to Him. Listen as He spreads the feast table before us and speaks His words of life.

"Come to Me.
All you who are weary and heavy laden and I will give you rest.
Take my yoke upon you and learn from me.
For I am gentle and humble in heart and you will find rest for your souls.

"I leave you with this invitation: come to Me.
Come and see.
Taste and see.
I am good.
Every good and every perfect gift comes down from the Father of lights with whom there is no shadow of turning.

"Ho. Everyone who thirsts. You who worry. You who are full of fear. You who are hungry.
Come.
Come to the waters.
Come to My fountain of life.
For I give freely.
You, who have no money, come buy and eat.

234 | CULTIVATING TRUST BY REBECCA van NOPPEN

Yes, come, buy wine and milk.

Without money and without price.

Why do you spend money for what is not bread, and your wages for what does not satisfy?

Listen carefully to Me and eat what is good, and let your soul delight itself in abundance.

Incline your ear, and come to Me.

Hear and your soul shall live.

"Come."

- Drawn from James 1:17, Isaiah 55:1-3, Revelation 21:6, Matthew 11:28-30, Genesis 3:8, Psalm 34:8, and Jeremiah 29:13

Let's bring our worries. Let's bring our fears. God is not afraid. He is not troubled. He will take all we bring to Him. He invites us to come and see, to ask, seek, and knock. We will find Him when we seek Him with all our hearts. He will not force us. He beckons us to a restored relationship provided through His death and resurrection. We have access to boldly come before Him, to drink, and eat, and find blessing because we have been chosen, adopted, redeemed, and called by name. We are no longer outside the garden of Eden. We are inside, back to the possibility of intimacy, walking with Him in the cool of the day.

God loves us beyond our worries, so do not fear. You have been made for such a time as this.

Come.

Confession, Repentance, & Forgiveness

On our journey of transformation, the gifts of confession, repentance, and forgiveness are keys to freedom. However, as my own children are learning these days, you can confess a sin or a shortcoming, but it doesn't mean you have repented and turned away from that sin.

God calls us to repentance—like washing our feet after a long, hard day walking the dusty roads of this world. We come back home at the end of the day and meet with Him. It's a gift. And as we consider repentance in light of our worries, fears, disbelief, and lack of trust, we can picture God welcoming us home each day, waiting at the end of the driveway, excited to see us return.

Abba, I confess.
Abba, I repent.
Abba, I receive your forgiveness.
Thank you.

It is as simple as these few words flowing from a heart of love for God.

It is that simple, but I have found I have had to learn to confess and repent as well as receive His forgiveness as part of the process. Sometimes I have just stopped at saying "sorry," but intentionally receiving His forgiveness has been, and continues to be, life transforming.

Digging Deeper: Refreshing Repentance

"Repent therefore and be converted, that your sins may be blotted out, so that times of refreshing may come from the presence of the Lord" (Acts 3:19, NKJV).

The Apostle Peter once spoke these words to a crowd of people who were among those who sent Jesus to the Cross: Jesus, the One who suffered and died and fulfilled the prophetic words of God by rising from the dead. Jesus the long-expected Messiah had come. With this great truth in his heart, Peter encouraged the crowd to believe and repent so that times of refreshing would come. With those words, he also spoke one of the greatest and often neglected truths of Scripture: repentance brings times of refreshing.

Ask anyone who has been cleansed from the guilt and shame of a life of sin by Jesus Christ. Repentance is a change of heart that brings revitalization and restoration. Refreshing in this context literally means "a recovery of breath."[1] Imagine running two miles uphill in torrential rains. At the top of the mountain you stop. You take a breath. The hard part is over. You can rest and be refreshed.

The same thing happens when we repent. Rest and recovery of breath follows in our entire being: mind, body, and soul find peace.

Repentance in our financial journey

Repentance in our financial journey is equally important and refreshing. When we find ourselves burdened with worry, fears, distrust, and bitterness, repentance draws us away from ourselves to the heart of the Father. It is an essential part of our financial journey.

Pastor Ray Borg, Ministry Liaison for Financial Discipleship Canada (www.notmine.ca), describes repentance as something that involves our thinking and our actions:

So what does repentance really mean? The word "**repent**" is made up of two Greek root words—"after" and "to think" and relates to a decision that results in a change of mind, which in turn leads to a change of purpose and action. It has to do with reflection upon, or reviewing our actions. It is a change of mind, to turn away from, and carries with it a sorrow or regret for unbelief and sin. It is the recognition of a true sense of guilt and sinfulness. It is having a hatred of sin and turning from it, to God. It results in a persistent desire and passion to lead a holy life in walking with God.

In other words, repentance simply means **to have a change of mind or heart.** It is a desire to move from sinning to not wanting to sin. It involves a change in action, behavior or attitude knowing that it is sin. In the area of financial management, we need to repent of ungodly attitudes or behaviours with regard to our money and possessions.

As Scripture says in Romans 7:19, "For what I do is not the good I want to do; no, the evil I do not want to do—this I keep on doing." As Christians we struggle with sin this side of eternity. By God's grace we are able to return to Him over and over again, and receive healing and cleansing through the shed blood of Jesus Christ and the finished work of the cross. The key aspect is to be intentional, with a sincere heart, to turn away from ungodly or sinful practices, thought life and belief systems.

Repentance is not merely saying to the Lord "I am sorry," but it is recognition that in some fashion we have grieved His heart and strayed from His intent and purposes for our lives. It recognizes the gentle work of the Holy Spirit bringing conviction in our lives, hitting the pause button, and taking time to reflect and ponder what the Holy Spirit is doing and speaking. It is recognition and acknowledgement that in some areas of our lives things are out of alignment with God's ways, whether it be in our thinking, attitudes or habits. In the area of finances, I may need to repent of a thought pattern that says, "I have had a tough day at work today and I deserve to have…" even though I know I do not have the resources to have those things.

Scripture in Romans 13:7 says, "Let no debt be outstanding." Maybe we need to repent of a **habit** of buying things whether we have the resources or not, because the issue really is about instant gratification. Or maybe we need to repent of putting our own needs ahead of the needs of our spouse and children.

MOVING FORWARD—REPENTANCE AS A JOURNEY OF TRANSFORMATION

Rev. Borg continues:

The journey of transformation and sanctification in all of our lives is under the Lord's leading and guidance. Altering unhealthy life-long habits and thinking also applies to the whole area of stewardship and, as in every other aspect of our lives, is an ongoing process on this side of heaven.

As you continue the journey of discovery in this area of stewardship, I encourage you to keep a heart that is always open to the leading and conviction of the Holy Spirit and always willing to repent when sin is revealed. Bringing the whole area of money and possessions under His Lordship involves the seeking out of further information from His word and from other sources, to gain understanding, insight and wisdom as well as practical tools and guidelines to manage this area of our lives. Given how much Scripture has to say about this topic, there is a need to be intentional and diligent in pursuit of transformation in this area.

Making changes in our daily activities, thought life, habits, and attitudes is not for the faint of heart. New disciplines, attitudes, habits, and at times lifestyle changes are

needed. Challenging our life-long belief systems can often be a threatening experience. However, persevering through, in repentance and action, is worth the effort.[2]

PRAYER OF REPENTANCE

As you have journeyed with the Lord learning about worry, money, and trust, perhaps issues have arisen that involve your finances but go beyond worry. You require a new path, a new way of thinking—a complete turn around. You may be sensing the conviction of the Holy Spirit over any number of actions, attitudes, or beliefs you have been living with around relationships, finances, or your heart allegiance.

It is as simple and as hard as these few words:

Abba, I confess.
Abba, I repent.
Abba, I receive your forgiveness.
Thank you.

However, if you are needing a bit more time, and a few more words to dig deeper in your time with the Lord, consider this sample prayer to help you get started.

Rev. Borg writes:
Once a sin or wrong attitude is recognized under the conviction of the Holy Spirit, one takes it to the Lord in prayer. It is acknowledging the sin and asking for the power of it to be broken over our lives. It involves requesting that the impact and pain it has caused to those closest to us be healed, alongside the restoration of relationships. Confession in a transparent fashion removes the power it has over us, bringing it into the light of His grace and mercy. A desire to genuinely take a new course of action is expressed before the Lord and a prayer is offered up to ask for strength and grace to walk a new journey ahead. This includes making new choices, holding ourselves accountable to spouses or others, and sincerely seeking to put the needs of the family and children before other wants and desires.[3]

Prayer:

Father, I thank You that I can come into Your Presence with confidence because of the sacrifice, death and resurrection of Your

Son Jesus Christ. Thank You that You have made a way for me in this season. Thank You that You alone are Lord. You are the Creator King, Almighty God, Gracious Father. And yet You have not been the Lord of my life in the area of finances. Often, I have put self on that throne.

I confess that I do not live with the truth of Your Lordship in my life. I confess that I put myself first. Thank You that Your word says that when I confess my sin, You are faithful and just, and forgive my unrighteous thinking and actions.

I ask that I would walk in Your strength to turn away from selfish, worldly thinking. I want You as Lord of my life and heart.

I confess that I have believed_____.
I have acted on those beliefs by_____.
I have trusted in _____
and I have not trusted in You or in Your word. I confess I have used th is_____ as a means to fill a need in my life, going to the world to find comfort and fulfillment. I confess that I have not sought You or Your word, to learn how to live according to Your way.

I repent of these thoughts and actions that have turned me away from You. I want to change this area of my life and I need You to break the power of these sins in my life. Break off the insecurities and fears that often lead me to make financial decisions that bring me into more trouble. When "old thinking" begins to rise up and I am tempted to fall back into these old, destructive patterns, help me look up to You, lifting my eyes to the hills. Keep me from falling again.

I ask You now, Holy Spirit, to meet the needs of my heart, both to be loved and comforted. Remind me of Your truth that You are my true Provider in all things. As I surrender my life, fill me afresh with Your truth that You are with me, and You are all I need. I receive Your forgiveness now, and I remain in Your presence in this sacred space to receive Your refreshing—this recovery of breath in my life. Thank You for all You are, Amen.

ACKNOWLEDGEMENTS

"Why do you boast in evil O mighty man? The goodness of God endures continually. But I am like a green olive tree in the house of God. I trust in the mercy of God forever and ever. I will praise you forever because you have done it. And in the Presence of Your saints I will wait on your name for it is good.

PSALM 52:1, 8-9 (NKJV)

I trust in God's mercy.
I wait on His name.
The goodness of God endures continually.

These three statements summarize how I feel after completing this project. This book was birthed in prayer and conversation with God. It has been a decade in the making. There were obstacles within myself that kept me from writing this book. Like many authors, I have had to overcome fears and thoughts of criticism and rejection. But more than that, I needed to be set free from my past so that I could embrace the new thing God wanted to do. I am so thankful to God for leading me through this project!

I want to thank my praying sisters: Debbie Gallagher, Danica Dixon, Bonnie Wallace, Monica Fife, Joanne Jehu, Natalie Skuce, Pam Dyck, and Shelly Horner. Some of us have been praying together for over a dozen years. Thank you from the bottom of my heart for all the love, support, and faith you pour into praying for MTE, our family, and this book.

I want to thank my "author companions" on this writing journey: Arlene Borg and Natalie Rowe. Your prayers, coaching, reading of the draft manuscript, and encouragement has kept me going. You are precious and beautiful to me!

I want to thank my sisters Mary Anne and Liz for walking with us, clothing us, blessing us, praying for us, and loving us—especially on this MTE journey. You have been the hands and feet of Jesus in our lives in so many ways. Liz—thanks for praying for a baby sister. So glad I could be the answer to your prayers :-) ! Not many people get to say that!

I want to thank Ray Borg for his friendship to us, his mentorship, and the many, many prayers he has prayed for us. You are a treasure, and a special gift of God to us. Thanks for joining us on the podcast every month and for your encouragement throughout the writing of this book.

Fred Brogan, God has used you in our lean times to keep us going. Thanks for investing in this book and being such a light of God in our lives.

Thank you Dave Froese and Shelley Spruit for putting your spiritual and agricultural insights into words. You have brought us truth and experience that have helped us understand this journey of cultivation much better.

I am so glad I have met new friends! Kim Driedger and Daylon C. Clark, and the team at Yairus Publishing House have been wonderful to work with. Your constant encouragement has been life-giving.

I also appreciate the time and work of Tim Bloedow in reading and editing the manuscript, as well as his wife Lynette who so faithfully loves and encourages me. I am so grateful for you both! Tim—your attention to detail has helped this become more than I imagined!

Mercedes. Wow! You are my first born, but you are also my writing companion. I never imagined that when I taught you to read and write all those years ago, you would now be the first reader of my first book. Thank you for your help with edits, clarifications, questions, and endnotes. The world of attributing sources has definitely changed in 30 years!

Zachary. Thank you so much for coming with your creativity and talent to capture the growth of trust from seedling to mature tree. Yes, I am so glad I had all you kids so I could use you in the future! :-)

To all of my beautiful children—Šarūnas, Mercedes, Zachary, Hope, Justus, and Serena—and special mention to Melissa! You have helped hold down the fort. You have encouraged me. You believed in me when I thought my writing didn't mean a thing. Thanks for doing dishes, making me laugh, and helping with technology over and over again. I love you to the beyond!

Thank you David for loving me for over 30 years. I would never have written this specific book if you hadn't answered the call to financial coaching—and, of course, dragged me with you :-) ! The wisdom you have shared and given to me whispers the wisdom of God in each word written. I hope you know how much your encouragement has meant in the writing of this project.

And finally, but most importantly, there is You. Father. Jesus. Spirit. I hope that the people who read what's written here will hear You, find You, and keep seeking You first and foremost. Obviously, I wouldn't have written any of these words apart from You and Your abundant love, wisdom, and gift giving. There aren't enough words to thank You for all You are and all You have done.

NOTES

PREFACE

1. Right Now Media. "Unleashed for the Gospel - Right Now Media." *YouTube*, uploaded by Right Now Media, 26 March 2013, https://www.youtube.com/watch?v=6YnG3jFkJwU&t=2s.

INTRODUCTION

1. Nouwen, Henri J. M. *The Return of the Prodigal Son - Anniversary Edition*. (New York: Random House Publishing, 2016) 212.

PRAYERS FOR THE JOURNEY

1. Claiborne, Shane and Jonathan Wilson-Hartgrove. Common *Prayer Pocket Edition - A Liturgy for Ordinary Radicals*. (Grand Rapids: Zondervan, 2012) 75.

WITH GOD

1. "Remembering Tulsa and Rethinking Prayer." *The Holy Post*. from Spotify, 2 June 2021, https://open.spotify.com/episode/6I2SN7E7pzbUOVYRJsvFHo?si=f0EuoV9EQdKmsLa4FqWQ-A&dl_branch=1.

WHAT IS WORRY?

1. Blue Letter Bible. "Merimneo." Blue Letter Bible, https://www.blueletterbible.org/lexicon/g3309/nkjv/tr/0-1/. Accessed 7 November 2020.

WHAT ARE YOU WORRIED ABOUT?

1. Cherry, Kendra. "The 5 Levels of Maslow's Hierarchy of Needs." Very Well Mind. https://www.verywellmind.com/what-is-maslows-hierarchy-of-needs-4136760. Accessed 20 March 2021.
2. Mcleod, Saul. "Maslow's Hierarchy of Needs." SimplyPsychology. https://www.simplypsychology.org/maslow.html. Accessed 20 March 2021.

CLOTHED WITH CHRIST

1. Eldredge, Stasi and John Eldredge. *Captivating: Unveiling the Mystery of a Woman's Soul*. (Nashville: Nelson Books, 2005) 17.

MORE THAN ENOUGH

1. Elevation Worship and Maverick City. "Jireh." YouTube, uploaded by

Elevation Worship, 26 March 2021 https://www.youtube.com/watch?v=mC-zw0zCCtg&ab_channel=ElevationWorship.

WORRY WEEDS

1. Dyck, Pam. *Soul Restored: Overcoming painful life struggles to find tremendous levels of freedom.* (Canada: Yairus Publishing, 2020) 167.
2. Dyck, Pam. *Soul Restored: Overcoming painful life struggles to find tremendous levels of freedom.* (Canada: Yairus Publishing, 2020) 167-168.
3. Dyck, Pam. *Soul Restored: Overcoming painful life struggles to find tremendous levels of freedom.* (Canada: Yairus Publishing, 2020) 168.
4. Dyck, Pam. *Soul Restored: Overcoming painful life struggles to find tremendous levels of freedom.* (Canada: Yairus Publishing, 2020) 168.
5. Dyck, Pam. *Soul Restored: Overcoming painful life struggles to find tremendous levels of freedom.* (Canada: Yairus Publishing, 2020) 169.

TODAY HAS ENOUGH TROUBLE

1. Nouwen, Henri J. M. *In the Name of Jesus - Reflections on Christian Leadership.* (New York: The Crossroad Publishing Company, 2015) 13.

PROVISION EVEN IN THE WINTER

1. Jobe, Kari and Cody Carnes. "The Blessing." *YouTube*, uploaded by WorshipHourVEVO, 24 March 2020. https://www.youtube.com/watch?v=amykXSyOG4o&ab_channel=WorshipHourVEVOWorshipHourVEVO
2. The Blessing. "The Blessing." *Youtube*, uploaded by The Blessing - Canada, 16 May 2020. https://www.youtube.com/watch?v=BSuwlEaQi54&ab_channel=TheBlessing-Canada

IN GOOD COMPANY

1. DiMarco, Kristene. "In Christ Alone." *YouTube*, uploaded by Bethel Music, 26 April, 2018. https://www.youtube.com/watch?v=UaHNKu3z2A4

YOU CANNOT SERVE TWO MASTERS

1. Borg, Ray and Jan Kupecz. *It's Not About the Money: unmasking mammon.* E-book, Financial Discipleship Canada, 2018.

2. Borg, Ray and Jan Kupecz. *It's Not About the Money: unmasking mammon.* (E-book, Financial Discipleship Canada, 2018.) 18-19.

3. Borg, Ray and Jan Kupecz. *It's Not About the Money: unmasking mammon.* (E-book, Financial Discipleship Canada, 2018.) 19.

4. Passini, Daniel. "20 More Powerful AW Tozer Quotes." Dr. Daniel Passini. https://danielpassini.org/20-more-powerful-aw-tozer-quotes/. Accessed 18 April, 2021.

SEEKING

1. Blue Letter Bible. "zēteō." Blue Letter Bible, https://www.blueletterbible.org/lexicon/g3309/nkjv/tr/0-1/. Accessed 9 February 2020.

2. Steppes of Faith. "The Difference between the Kingdom of GOd and the Kingdom of Heaven." Steppes of Faith, https://steppesoffaith-56895.medium.com/the-difference-between-the-kingdom-of-god-and-the-kingdom-of-heaven-dfcdbaf6b0e3. Accessed 23 May 2021.

3. "What is the difference between the Kingdom of God and the Kingdom of Heaven?" GotQuestions.org. https://www.gotquestions.org/kingdom-heaven-God.html. Accessed 23 May 2021.

4. Jethani, Skye. *What if Jesus Was Serious?* (Chicago: Moody Publishers, 2020) 25.

5. Jethani, Skye. *What if Jesus Was Serious?* (Chicago: Moody Publishers, 2020) 107.

6. Comer, John Mark. The Ruthless Elimination of Hurry: How to Stay Emotionally Healthy and Spiritually Alive in the Chaos of the Modern World. (E-book: Waterbrook, 2019) 77.

7. Comer, John Mark. The Ruthless Elimination of Hurry: How to Stay Emotionally Healthy and Spiritually Alive in the Chaos of the Modern World. (E-book: Waterbrook, 2019) 82.

TREASURES WORTH SEEKING

1. Groban, Josh. "You are Loved (Don't Give Up)." *YouTube*, uploaded by Josh Groban, 14 February 2010. https://www.youtube.com/watch?v=EGLSk3AVcUU&ab_channel=JoshGroban.

TREASURES WORTH SEEKING: SIDE BAR

1. Jethani, Skye. *What if Jesus Was Serious?* Chicago, Moody Publishers, 2020.

2. Jethani, Skye. *What if Jesus Was Serious?* (Chicago: Moody Publishers, 2020) 106-107.

THROWING GLITTER

1. Gadd, Ashlee. *Ashlee Gadd*. 2021. https://www.ashleegadd.com/. Accessed 9 May 2021.

2. Gadd, Ashlee. "On Throwing Glitter and a few other good things." 2021 https://view.flodesk.com/emails/5fa9dc946996343cd67bf568?fbclid=IwAR2wd 2gxOlnD0V-5y6e8C4IEKl5VnNnqjIkMOryIsdPptYR7CemA_Yuvzlc Accessed 9 May 2021.

3. "Arrow Leadership." Arrow Leadership, https://www.arrowleadership.org/. Accessed 9 November 2020.

GOOD EYES

1. Jethani, Skye. *What if Jesus Was Serious?* (Chicago: Moody Publishers, 2020) 111.

2. Jethani, Skye. *What if Jesus Was Serious?* (Chicago: Moody Publishers, 2020) 111.

3. "What did Jesus mean when He said "the eye is the lamp of the body"?" GotQuestions.org. https://www.gotquestions.org/kingdom-heaven-God.html. Accessed 16 February 2021.

REMEMBER YOUR CREATOR - SIDEBAR

1. Gibson, David. *Living Life Backward*. (Wheaton: Crossway, 2017) 141.

2. Gibson, David. *Living Life Backward*. (Wheaton: Crossway, 2017) 140.

WORSHIP WHAT YOU LOVE

1. Smith, James K. A. *You Are What You Love - The Spiritual Power of Habit*. Grand Rapids, Brazos Press, 2016.

2. Smith, James K. A. *You Are What You Love - The Spiritual Power of Habit*. (Grand Rapids: Brazos Press, 2016) 23-24.

3. Brown, Steve A. *Leading Me: Eight Practices for a Christian Leader's Most Important Assignment. (Belleville: Castle Quay Books, 2015)* 64.

4. Smith, James K. A. *You Are What You Love - The Spiritual Power of Habit*. (Grand Rapids: Brazos Press, 2016) 37.

5. Smith, James K. A. *You Are What You Love - The Spiritual Power of Habit*. (Grand Rapids: Brazos Press, 2016) 23-24.

6. Smith, James K. A. *You Are What You Love - The Spiritual Power of Habit*. (Grand Rapids: Brazos Press, 2016) 71-72.

A MEANDERING PATH: FROM WORRY TO PRAYER
1. Eldredge, John. *Moving Mountains: Praying with Passion, Confidence and Authority*. (Nashville: Thomas Nelson, 2016) 26.

NAVIGATING THE OBSTACLES
1. Yairus House [@yairushouse]. "Obstacles are sometimes the best opportunities!" Instagram, May 29, 2021, https://www.instagram.com/p/CPd3KLFFgqc/?utm_medium=copy_link.
2. TobyMac. "Help is on the Way (Maybe Midnight)." YouTube, uploaded by TobyMac, 19 February 2021.
3. TobyMac. "Help is on the Way (Maybe Midnight)." YouTube, uploaded by TobyMac, 19 February 2021.
4. Johnson, Ben. "Evacuation of Dunkirk." Historic UK, https://www.historic-uk.com/HistoryUK/HistoryofBritain/Evacuation-of-Dunkirk/. Accessed 20 May 2021.
5. King George VI. "Day of prayer The King." YouTube, uploaded by Bruce Reekie, 31 August 2018. https://www.youtube.com/watch?v=nBIiZqrtuk8&ab_channel=BruceReekie.
6. Harding, Carla. "The Miracle of Dunkirk." Lectio365 App, 4 June 2021, https://www.24-7prayer.com/dailydevotional

HE WILL SEE TO IT
1. Blue Letter Bible. "yᵉhōvâ yir'ê." Blue Letter Bible, https://www.blueletterbible.org/lang/lexicon/lexicon.cfm?Strongs=H3070&t=NKJV. Accessed 7 March 2021.

ALWAYS REJOICE
1. Nouwen, Henri. "Henri Nouwen Quotes About Joy." AZ Quotes, https://www.azquotes.com/author/10905-Henri_Nouwen/tag/joy. Accessed 29 May 2021.

LAMENT
1. Doerksen, Brian. "Psalm 13 (How Long O Lord)". YouTube, uploaded by milordsheep, 14 July 2014. https://www.youtube.com/

watch?v=mbcE2HRhyrQ&ab_channel=milordsheep.

2. WTC Theology. "Brian Doerksen - Lament & Christian Worship." YouTube, uploaded by WTC Theology, 18 March 2014. https://www.youtube.com/watch?v=2uB9b3QaTTY.

3. Rah, Soong-Chan. *Prophetic Lament, A Call for Justice in Troubled Times.* (Illinois: InterVarsity Press, 2015) 23.

THE SWEATER

1. Garlough Brown, Shannon. *Sensible Shoes: A Story about the Spiritual Journey.* (Illinois: InterVarsity Press Books, 2013) 80.

IT'S NOT MINE

1. "Arrow Leadership." Arrow Leadership, https://www.arrowleadership.org/. Accessed 9 November 2020.

SURROUNDED

1. Smith, Michael W. "Surrounded (Fight My Battles)". YouTube, uploaded by Michael W. Smith, 29 December 2017. https://www.youtube.com/watch?v=YBl84oZxnJ4.

START AT THE END

1. Gibson, David. *Living Life Backward.* (Wheaton: Crossway, 2017) 129.
2. Gibson, David. *Living Life Backward.* (Wheaton: Crossway, 2017) 12.
3. Gibson, David. *Living Life Backward.* (Wheaton: Crossway, 2017) 126.
4. Gibson, David. *Living Life Backward.* (Wheaton: Crossway, 2017) 19.

GOING FORWARD: LET'S TALK MONEY - TOGETHER

1. Smallbone, Joel and Luke Smallbone. "Together." YouTube, uploaded by for KING & COUNTRY, 4 May 2020. https://www.youtube.com/watch?v=lR1Hk0FVi_k.
2. Smallbone, Joel and Luke Smallbone. "Together." YouTube, uploaded by for KING & COUNTRY, 4 May 2020. *https://www.youtube.com/watch?v=lR1Hk0FVi_k.*

CONFESSION, REPENTANCE, & FORGIVENESS

1. Blue Letter Bible. "anapsyxis." Blue Letter Bible, https://www.blueletterbible.org/lexicon/g403/nkjv/tr/0-1/. Accessed 15 February 2021.

2. Borg, Ray. *Unleashed Session 4: Commitment*. 3 May 2021, More Than Enough Financial.

3. Borg, Ray. *Unleashed Session 4: Commitment*. 3 May 2021, More Than Enough Financial.

Rebecca van Noppen
Communicator - Writer - Podcast Host - Friend

Rebecca is a communicator and writer, working alongside her husband David in their business More Than Enough Financial. Her desire is to see people draw close to God's heart, as they discover God's purposes for them on their financial journeys. As co-host of the "Let's Talk Money with Dave and Reb" podcast, she has a passion to declare God's hope and freedom to people bound by financial blame, harmful behaviours and the shame and embarrassment that comes as a result. She longs to hear people talk about money in helpful, life-giving ways, and loves to be part of those conversations.

Rebecca and David have been married 30 years, and their family of five children plus in-laws keeps on growing. They live with three of their children, and one dog, on 25 acres of beautiful bush land in Eastern Ontario. Rebecca loves long drives, beach vacations, good books, cutting firewood, knitting socks, crocheting blankets, and sitting with friends around an open fire. If you come to visit and can't find her inside, you will likely find her on the back porch talking to God with a nice cup of tea in hand.

**More
than
Enough**

FINANCIAL
FITNESS

To learn more about Rebecca's business, please check out:
M O R E T H A N E N O U G H . C A

To purchase more books or for bulk orders, please visit:
M O R E T H A N E N O U G H B O O K S . C O M

YAIRUS

PUBLISHING
HOUSE

You were made to share what you know.
If you have ever taught someone anything...

You can write a book!

We'd love to chat. Get started today at:

YAIRUS.COM